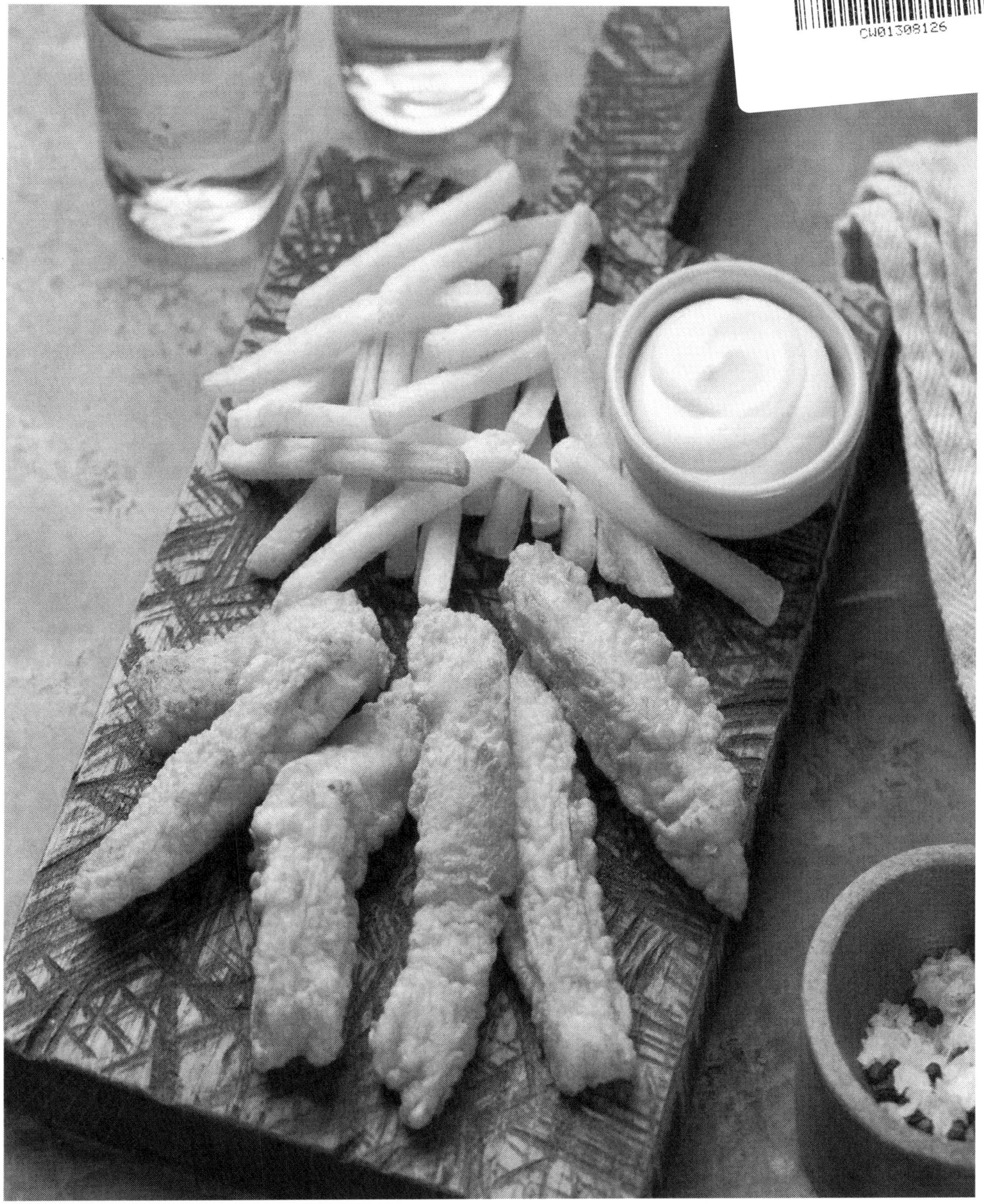

The Ultimate Air Fryer Cookbook UK:

Have Fun Preparing Simple, Inexpensive Recipes That Will Make Your Guests' Mouths Water

Tom Rinald

© Copyright 2023 - All rights reserved.

Table of Contents

Introduction 9

Chapter 1: A First-Timer's Guide to Air Fryer 10

Breakfast Recipes 14

    Mozzarella Chives Omelet 14

    Chicken Casserole with Almonds 15

    Mushroom Frittata with Mozzarella Cheese 15

    Cheddar Broccoli Quiche 16

    Cheddar Frittata 17

    Mozzarella Soufflé with Ham 17

    Cheddar Mushroom Taquitos 18

    Mozzarella Vegetable Frittata 19

    Breakfast Egg and Sausage Burrito 20

    Vanilla French Toast Sticks 21

    Breakfast Muffins with Bacon and Cheese 22

    Home-Made Potatoes with Paprika 23

    Crispy Parmesan Asparagus 24

    Air-Fried Chicken Wings and Waffles 24

    Cheddar Tater Tot with Sausage 25

    Tasty Hash Browns with Radish 26

    Egg-Cilantro Cups 27

Feta Stuffed Peppers with Broccoli 28

Zucchini Muffins with Cinnamon 29

Mushroom Frittata 30

Simple Cheddar-Omelet 30

Strawberry Tarts 31

Italian Frittata with Feta Cheese 32

Strawberry and Peach Toast 33

Flavorful Scrambled Eggs with Chorizo 33

Spinach Frittata with Mozzarella 34

Awesome Everything Bagels 35

Sweet Berry Muffins 36

Creamy Soufflés 37

Egg Soufflé with Mushroom and Broccoli 38

Meat Recipes 39

Kansas City's Baby Back Rib Recipe 39

Top Round Roast With Herbs Blend 40

Pork In Garlic Sauce 41

Peanut Sauce With Flavorsome Pork Chops 42

Loin Chops With Za'atar Lamb 43

Short Loin Steak With Grilled Mayo 43

Potatoes With Pork Loin 44

Dill Pickles With Smoked Brisket 45

Worcester Meatloaf 45

Wine Marinated Flank Steak 46

Pork Roulade 47

Old-Fashioned Beef Burgers 48

Beef Jerky 48

Vegetables With Hearty Beef Cubes 49

Buttered Strip Loin Steak 50

Buttered Garlic-Celery With Roast Beef 50

Smoked Pork 51

Cumin Lamb Kebabs, Sichuan And Caraway 51

Hot Paprika Beef 52

Hot Bacon Bites 52

Beef Schnitzel 53

Sage Sauce Recipe With Pork Chops 53

Meatball Sausage 54

Ghee Mushroom With Beef Mix 55

Cumin-Paprika With Beef Brisket 56

Fish and Seafood Recipes 57

Asian Swordfish 57

Tilapia Sandwiches with Tartar Sauce 58

Quick Shrimp Skewers 59

Crispy Fish Sticks 60

Mustard-Crusted Fish Fillets 60

Rockfish with Avocado Cream 61

Cayenne Flounder Cutlets 62

Shrimp Scampi 63

Sole and Asparagus Bundles 64

Tuna-Stuffed Quinoa Patties 65

Country Shrimp 66

Steamed Cod with Garlic and Swiss Chard 67

Cucumber and Salmon Salad 68

Dukkah-Crusted Halibut 69

Scallops with Asparagus and Peas 70

Appetizer& Snacks Recipes 71

Roasted Cashews 71

Beef Taquitos 73

Persimmon Chips 74

Carrot Chips 74

Potato Chips 75

Corn on the Cob 76

Air Fryer Ravioli 77

Sweet Potato Fries	78
Pasta Chips	78
Avocado Fries	79
Fiesta Chicken Fingers	80

Vegetarian & Vegan Recipes 81

Broccoli Stuffed With Cheese And Pepper	81
Healthy Veggie Rice	82
Sweet And Spicy Tofu	83
Delicious Vegan Calzone	84
Tofu Ala Italian	85
Stuffed Eggplant With A Twist	86
Glazed Carrots	87
Veggies Air-Fried Sushi	87
Drizzling Onion	88
Eggplant Potato And Zucchini Chips	89
Baked Potato And Parsnip	90
Cheesy Pizza With A Crust Made Of Broccoli	91

Dessert Recipes 92

Apple Pastries	92
Blueberry Hand Pies	93
Brownie Bars	94

Vanilla Soufflé 96

Chocolate Chip Cookie 97

Air Fried Butter Cake 98

Shortbread Fingers 99

Conclusion **100**

Appendix 1 Measurement Conversion Chart **101**

Introduction

The first recipe I tried is still fresh in my mind. It was a simple air fryer potato wedges, and after that, I was powerless to stop.

You'll be surprised at the variety of food magic an air fryer can create; most people assume that French fries are the only thing that can be cooked in one.

Without having to keep track of calories, you may have all the delicious things you want, including bagels, poultry, and even hard-boiled eggs.

In addition to turning most unhealthy foods healthier, an air fryer has so many applications that, given enough time, it virtually entirely replaces your oven!

We recognize that many individuals want to join the "air fryer gang," but they are unsure on how to get started or what to buy. Because of this, you must learn everything in this first page to determine whether purchasing an air fryer is worthwhile.

Chapter 1:
A First-Timer's Guide to Air Fryer

What Is an Air Fryer?

An air fryer is a countertop convection oven that is designed to simulate deep frying. It has a fan and exhaust system that blows hot air and provides crispy frying flavor and evenly cooks and browns food without oil or fat.

It's convenient and super easy to use, and you can cook food in less time. Unlike an oven, it preheats quickly and can be versatile. For more advanced air fryers, you can get different functional buttons like fry, toast, bagel, etc, giving you tons of options to experiment with.

There are different criteria to consider when buying an air fryer, such as capacity, complexity, size, etc. It largely depends on what your budget is and what you plan to do with your air fryer.

Although there are loads of air fryer brands to choose from, there are just two major types of air fryers - Basket type and Oven type.

Basket Type

The basket type is the more popular one and it has a kind of wide drawer like compartment that serves as the basket in which food is cooked.

It comes in two different sizes, the small and the large. The small size ranges from 2.7 quarts to 3.7 quarts while the large sizes are between 4 quarts to 7 quarts.

The baskets also come in just two shapes. If it isn't round shaped, then it's square shaped.

Oven Type

Don't get confused! The air fryer oven is clearly different from a normal oven that has an air fryer function. They look more like a microwave or even a toaster oven, and instead of a basket, it has racks like a regular oven. Most air fryer ovens even come with a rotisserie chicken rod.

If compared, the basket style air fryer seems to cook a little bit faster than the air fryer oven.

How Do the Air Fryers Work?

Inbuilt fans in air fryers circulate hot air to cook food in a deep-fried fashion without drenching it in oil.

The cooking chamber of the air fryer produces heat from all directions by convective heat from a strong air stream moving upward from the open bottom of the food chamber and radiant heat from the heating element above the food. Without idle air circulation like in a convection oven, little quantities of hot air are forced to flow over the surface of the heater and over the meal. The airflow is then directed to the food's bottom through a molded guide. In plain English, the air fryer has a fan and heating system that circulates hot air around the cooking basket or tray from the top and bottom compartments.

Food cooks and browns evenly thanks to the frying effect produced by the swift air flow. Additionally, the heat drastically cuts down on cooking time while maintaining the inner and exterior crispiness of the meal.

For more precise cooking, most air fryers typically incorporate built-in temperature and timer settings. Food is prepared in a basket or rack on a drip tray so that the heat may penetrate and evenly cook all of its surfaces.

Additionally, some air fryers have straightforward preset cooking settings for foods including fish, steak, chicken, cake, shrimp, beef, and fries.

Following are crucial pointers that will help cooking with an air fryer considerably simpler now that we all realize these.

Important Tips to Keep in Mind

- Never forget the grate in the basket
  Using the grate allows hot air to go round the food and keeps the food from sitting in excess oil.
- Check the condition of the food frequently
  During the cooking process, always remember to pull out the basket to see how it is doing. To properly brown the food, take the basket out every one to two minutes. There is no need to turn off the machine because it will automatically shut off when the basket is removed.
- Be careful!
  One of the benefits of using an air fryer is that the food cooks faster than you think. Although air fryers usually have cooking time and temperature manuals for different foods, you need to start with the lowest possible time and continue to increase the cooking time until you achieve the desired result.
  Also, the less food you have in the basket, the shorter the cooking time. The more food you have, the longer it will take.
- Preheat your air fryer
  Although not absolutely necessary, it will reduce your cooking time. Usually, this shouldn't take much time, about two to three minutes, so you can turn your air fryer on just before you're ready to start cooking.
- Never overcrowd your air fryer basket
  Overcrowding your air fryer basket is usually a bad idea. When you put too much in your air fryer basket, your food is likely to steam instead of air fry, leaving you with soggy food. The best you can do is to split, and air fry your food in batches. It may take longer but you will love the result.
- Use foil.

Having to clean up after every use can seem like a daunting task to many. To reduce the stress, you can line the bottom of your air fryer's basket with foil or parchment paper so that you'll have less to worry about cleanup. This is especially useful when you're cooking something that has plenty of sauce or spices which would otherwise drip and fly around the machine. Just make sure the food you're cooking has enough weight to hold down the paper or foil so that it doesn't fly around in the machine once you turn it on.

- Drippings = extra flavor
  Remember the drippings that gathered at the bottom of your air fryer when you prepared greasy food? Yes, that one!
- You do not have to throw it away because those drippings are full of flavor, so they can be used to make gravies, sauces, or even marinades. Make sure to save those drippings so you can use them to make your next meal even more delicious.
- Use heat-resistant materials only.
  Keeping your air fryer away from anything that easily burns or melts and placing it near materials that are heat-resistant are absolutely necessary ideas to adhere to. The surface top must be heat- resistant, like a marble countertop. Make sure the vent isn't blowing onto anything that can burn or melt, like plastic.
- Always Refer To Your Manual

Breakfast Recipes

1. Mozzarella Chives Omelet

- 6 eggs, whisked.
- 8 fl.oz chives, chopped.
- Cooking spray
- 8 fl.oz mozzarella, shredded.
- To taste, add black pepper and salt.

PREP

1. Grease the right baking pan with cooking spray.
2. Add the whisked eggs, chopped chives, shredded mozzarella, salt, and pepper to a medium bowl.
3. Pour the egg mixture into the prepared pan, then spread it out.
4. In your air fryer, cook for 20 minutes at 350 degrees Fahrenheit (175 degrees Celsius).
5. Put the meal on plates after cooking.

Per serving:

- Kcal: 119; Fat: 8g; Carbs: 1g; Net Carbs: 0g; Protein: 10.7g

2. Chicken Casserole with Almonds

- 59 ml almonds, chopped.
- 4 fl. oz almond milk
- 4 eggs, whisked.
- 8 fl.oz chicken meat, cooked and shredded.
- 2.5 ml oregano, dried
- Cooking spray

PREP

1. Grease a suitable baking pan with cooking spray.
2. Combine the whisked eggs and the remaining ingredients in a medium bowl.
3. After pouring the ingredients onto the baking sheet, spread them out.
4. 350 degrees F/175 degrees C for 25 minutes of air frying.
5. Cooked food should be served warmly on platters.

Per serving:

- Kcal: 233; Fat: 17.1g; Carbs: 3g; Protein: 17.6g

3. Mushroom Frittata with Mozzarella Cheese

- 5 eggs
- 3 sliced mushrooms
- 1 bell pepper, sliced, 30 mls melted butter, 8 fl.oz shredded mozzarella cheese
- 15 ml arugula for serving with black pepper
- 15 ml of salt

PREP

1. Prepare each ingredient listed in the recipe.
2. Slice and wash your vegetables. Moreover, beat the eggs. Get the cheese grated.
3. Before adding the ingredients to the air fryer basket, melted butter is mixed with the mushrooms, black pepper, and green onions. Aim for a cooking temperature of about 350 °F/175 °C and cook for five minutes. Shake the basket twice.
4. Combine the eggs, grated mozzarella, salt, and black pepper in the proper bowl while the other steps are being completed. Pour the egg mixture on top of the vegetables.
5. Place the dish in the preheated air fryer, and cook for 5 minutes, or until the eggs are set, at a temperature of almost 350°F/175°C.
6. Toss in some arugula.

Per serving:

- Kcal: 167; Fat: 12.7g; Carbs: 4.7g; Protein: 10g

4. Cheddar Broccoli Quiche

- 8 small broccoli florets
- 2 eggs
- 4 fl. oz of heavy cream
- 30 mls of cheddar, grated
- Black pepper and salt, to taste

PREP

1. At 325 degrees F/ 160 degrees C, preheat your air fryer.
2. Grease 2 5-inch ceramic dishes with oil or cooking spray.
3. Put eggs, salt, heavy cream, and black pepper into a suitable mixing bowl.
4. Whisk it well then put broccoli florets on the dish's bottom and pour the egg mixture over them.
5. Cook it at 325 degrees F/ 160 degrees C for almost 10 minutes.
6. Serve warm.

Per serving:

- Kcal: 303; Fat: 17.2g; Carbs: 25g; Net Carbs: 16g; Protein: 18.1g

5. Cheddar Frittata

- 4 eggs
- 4 fl. oz of cooked and chopped sausage
- 4 fl. oz of shredded cheddar cheese
- 1 chopped green onion
- 30 mls of chopped red bell pepper
- 1 pinch of cayenne powder

PREP

1. Set your air fryer to 350 degrees F/175 degrees C.
2. Grease a decent 6-inch cake pan with cooking spray or a little oil.
3. In a good basin, whisk eggs.
4. Stir to thoroughly blend before adding the sausage, bell pepper, onion, cheese, and cayenne.
5. Place the prepared egg mixture in the cake pan and cook for nearly 20 minutes in the preheated air fryer.
6. Include any fresh veggies and greens while serving. Happy eating, Frittata!

Per serving:

- Kcal: 291; Carbs: 10.7g; Protein: 20.1g

6. Mozzarella Soufflé with Ham

- 6 eggs
- 1/3 cup milk
- Shredded mozzarella cheese, one-half cup
- 1 heaping tablespoon of recently minced parsley
- 15 ml of salt
- 4 fl. oz of diced ham
- Black pepper, 15 ml
- Garlic powder, 1/2 teaspoon

PREP

1. Spray nonstick cooking spray on 4 ramekins. Set your air fryer to 350 degrees F/175 degrees C.
2. Add all the ingredients to a good bowl, and stir until everything is thoroughly combined.

3. Put the buttered ramekins inside your air fryer after pouring the egg mixture into them.
4. For 8 minutes, cook it in your air fryer.
5. The soufflé should then be carefully removed from the air fryer and left to cool.
6. Dispense and savor!

Per serving:

- Kcal: 145; Carbs: 2g; Net Carbs: 0.5g; Protein: 12.9g

7. Cheddar Mushroom Taquitos

- 8 whole-wheat tortillas
- 2–3 king oyster mushrooms
- 8 fl.oz of shredded cheddar cheese
- 15ml of lime juice
- ⅛ cup of olive oil
- ¼ tablespoon of chili powder
- 15 ml of ground cumin
- 15 ml of paprika
- 2.5 ml of dried oregano
- 2.5 ml of garlic powder
- 1 ml of salt
- 1 ml of black pepper
- 1 ml of onion powder

PREP

1. The oyster mushrooms must be cleaned before use.
2. Cut them lengthwise into 1/8-inch-thick pieces.
3. Combine the chili, cumin, paprika, oregano, garlic, salt, black pepper, and onion powder in a large mixing basin.
4. Add the oil and lime juice and stir.
5. To the basin containing the sliced mushroom, add the spice combination.
6. 350°F/175°C should be the temperature setting for your air fryer.
7. The mushroom should be air-cooked in the air fryer for around 7 to 10 minutes.
8. All of the tortillas should be topped with the sautéed mushrooms.
9. Add shredded cheese and make a thin roll from each stuffed tortilla.
10. Spray all rolled tortillas with some oil and Air fry for almost 10 minutes.

Per serving:

- Kcal: 150; Carbs: 13g; Protein: 5.1g

8. Mozzarella Vegetable Frittata

- 1 chopped tiny onion
- 2 garlic cloves
- ⅓ pack (4 ounces) spinach 3 beaten eggs and 3 ounces shredded mozzarella
- Olive oil, 15 ml
- Black pepper and salt

PREP

1. Your air fryer should be preheated to 370 degrees F, or 185 degrees C. In a baking pan, oil should be heated for approximately one minute.
2. The diced onions and garlic cloves should be added to the pan and sautéed for two to three minutes.
3. Spinach should be added to a half-Air fry and cooked for three to five minutes.
4. In the proper bowl, whisk the beaten eggs with salt and black pepper. Add the ingredients to a baking dish.
5. Warm up the air fryer, place the pan inside, and air fried it for 6 to 8 minutes, or until the food is cooked.
6. Sprinkle cheese till soft after 2 minutes.

Per serving:

- Kcal: 282; Carbs: 6g; Net Carbs: 2.5g; Protein: 19.3g

9. Breakfast Egg and Sausage Burrito

- 6 eggs
- Black pepper and salt
- frying fluid
- Chopped red bell pepper, half a cup.
- Chopped green bell pepper, half a cup.
- 8 ounces of chicken sausage, ground
- 4 fl. oz salsa
- 8-inch medium flour tortillas, six
- Shredded Cheddar cheese in a half-cup.

PREP

1. Grease the air fryer basket and heat your air fryer to 400 degrees F/205 degrees C.
2. In a suitable bowl, whisk the eggs. To taste, add salt and black pepper.
3. Cook eggs, veggies, ground beef, and oil in a skillet for 10 minutes.
4. Cover the tortillas with this mixture, then sprinkle cheese and salsa over top.
5. After rolling the tortillas, put the burritos in the greased air fryer basket.

Per serving:

- Kcal: 162; Carbs: 13g; Net Carbs: 7g; Protein: 9.7g

10. Vanilla French Toast Sticks

- 4 slices Texas toast
- 15ml butter
- 1 egg
- 15 ml stevia
- 15 ml ground cinnamon
- 59 ml milk
- 15 ml vanilla extract
- Cooking oil

PREP

1. Bread should be cut into sticks and set aside.
2. In a large broad basin, combine the remaining ingredients for the dish.
3. Pre-heat your air fryer to 400 degrees F or 205 degrees C.
4. Breadsticks should be dipped in the prepared egg mixture before being placed in the air fryer.
5. The bread sticks were air-fried for ten minutes.
6. Serve.

Per serving:

- Kcal: 102; Carbs: 13g; Net Carbs: 7g; Protein: 3.3g

11. Breakfast Muffins with Bacon and Cheese

- Prep Time: 15 minutes | Serves: 4

INGREDIENTS

- 12 fl. oz of all-purpose flour
- 10 ml of baking powder
- 4 fl. oz of milk
- 2 eggs
- 15ml of freshly chopped parsley
- 4 cooked and chopped bacon slices
- 1 thinly chopped onion
- 4 fl. oz of shredded cheddar cheese
- 2.5 ml of onion powder
- 15 ml of salt
- 15 ml of black pepper

PREP

1. Pre-heat your air fryer to 360 degrees F or 180 degrees C.
2. Add all the ingredients to a good bowl, and stir until everything is thoroughly combined.
3. Then either line the muffin tins with parchment paper or oil them with nonstick cooking spray. Pour the batter into each muffin cup in an appropriate amount.
4. Put it inside your air fryer and cook it there for nearly 15 minutes.
5. Thereafter, carefully remove it from your air fryer and allow it to chill.

Per serving:

- Kcal: 290; Carbs: 42g; Net Carbs: 18g; Protein: 12.6g

12. Home-Made Potatoes with Paprika

- Prep Time: 15 minutes | Cook time: 25 minutes | Serves: 4

INGREDIENTS

- 3 large russet potatoes
- 15ml canola oil
- 15ml extra-virgin olive oil
- 15 ml paprika
- Salt
- Black pepper
- 8 fl.oz chopped onion
- 8 fl.oz chopped red bell pepper
- 8 fl.oz chopped green bell pepper

PREP

1. Potatoes should be cut into 1-inch chunks.
2. The potatoes should soak for between 30 and 60 minutes in a good dish of cold water.
3. Dry the potatoes off before giving them a good paper towel wipe. 4. Put them back in the bare basin.
4. To flavor, mix in the paprika, canola and olive oils, black pepper, and salt. 6. Toss the potatoes to evenly coat them.
5. Enter the air fryer with the potatoes.
6. Cook for 20 minutes while rotating the air fryer basket four times, once every five minutes.
7. Place the red, green, and onion in the air fryer basket. Cook the potatoes for a further 3 to 4 minutes, or until they are tender and the black pepper is soft.
8. Prior to serving, cool.

Per serving:

- Kcal: 275; Carbs: 48g; Net Carbs: 30g; Protein: 5.4g

13. Crispy Parmesan Asparagus

- Serves: 4

INGREDIENTS

- 1 pound asparagus spears
- 30 mls butter
- 4 fl. oz Parmesan cheese, grated.
- Salt/Black pepper
- 15 ml lemon zest

PREP

1. Prepare all the ingredients for the recipe. Peel, wash, and dry the asparagus.
2. After sprinkling the asparagus stalks with salt and black pepper, add butter.
3. They should be cooked for 8 to 10 minutes at a temperature of 370 degrees Fahrenheit/185 degrees Celsius in a deep air fryer basket. Shake the container a bit while it's cooking.
4. Serve with lemon zest and parmesan.

Per serving:

- Kcal: 85; Carbs: 4.5g; Protein: 3.7g

14. Air-Fried Chicken Wings and Waffles

- Serves: 4

INGREDIENTS

- 8 entire wing chickens
- 20 ml of garlic powder
- Rub or spice for chicken
- 4 fl. oz. of all-purpose flour, black pepper
- frying fluid
- 8 iced waffles
- maple sugar

PREP

1. Your air fryer should be preheated to 400 degrees F, or 205 degrees C.
2. Place the chicken in a bowl and season to taste with black pepper, chicken spice, and garlic powder.
3. Add the chicken, sealable plastic bag, and flour. To thoroughly coat the chicken, give it a good shake.
4. Cooking oil ought to be used to lubricate the air fryer basket.
5. In the oiled air fryer basket, chicken should be air-fried for 20 minutes, flipping once or twice.
6. Frozen waffles should be added to the air fryer and cooked for around 6 minutes before being removed and placed on a dish.
7. Serve waffles alongside the air-fried chicken.

Per serving:

- Kcal: 423; Carbs: 64g; Protein: 11.9g

15. Cheddar Tater Tot with Sausage

- Prep Time: 15 minutes | Cook time: 20 minutes | Serves: 4

INGREDIENTS

- 4 eggs
- 8 ounces of milk
- 20 ml of onion powder
- Black pepper and salt
- frying fluid
- 12 ounces of chicken sausage, ground
- frozen tater tots, one pound
- shred 177 ml Cheese, cheddar

PREP

1. Combine the milk, onion powder, black pepper, salt, and eggs in a bowl.
2. Cooking oil should be used to coat a good skillet, and it should be heated on medium-high.
3. Add the ground sausage and cook it in the pan for 4 minutes.
4. Grease a barrel pan with frying oil to prepare it.
5. Spread the tater tots out in the prepared barrel pan. Air frying for almost six minutes.
6. Simmer for a further 6 minutes after adding the egg and sausage combination.
7. Grate the cheese and sprinkle it on the potato tot.

8. Cook for a further 2 to 3 minutes. 9. Before serving, chill.

Per serving:

- Kcal: 181;Carbs: 4g; Protein: 12.9g

16. Tasty Hash Browns with Radish

- Serves: 4

INGREDIENTS

- 1-pound radishes, washed and cut off roots
- 15ml olive oil
- 2.5 ml paprika
- 2.5 ml onion powder
- 2.5 ml garlic powder
- 1 medium onion
- 1 ml black pepper
- 7.5 ml salt

PREP

1. Cut radishes and onion with a mandolin slicer.
2. Sliced onion, radishes, and stir with olive oil in a medium mixing bowl.
3. The air fryer basket should be filled with onion and radish slices, which should be cooked for 8 minutes at about 360 degrees F/180 degrees C. Shake the basket twice.
4. Returning the onion and radish slices to the proper mixing basin, season them.
5. Slices of onion and radish should be cooked in the air fryer basket once more for 5 minutes at 400 degrees F/205 degrees C. Shake the basket after the halfway mark.
6. After serving, indulge.

Per serving:

- Kcal: 62; Carbs: 7.1g; Net Carbs: 1g; Protein: 1.2g

17. Egg-Cilantro Cups

- Prep Time: 15 minutes | Cook time: 14 minutes | Serves: 4

INGREDIENTS

- 4 eggs
- chopped cilantro, 15 ml.
- Four tablespoons of half-and-half
- 8 fl. oz. of shredded cheddar cheese.
- 8 fl. oz. of diced veggies.
- roasted pepper
- Salt

PREP

1. Spray cooking spray on 4 ramekins, then place them aside.
2. Combine eggs, cilantro, half-and-half, vegetables, 4 oz. cheese, salt, black pepper, and other seasonings in a good mixing dish.
3. The egg mixture should be put into the 4 ramekins.
4. In the air fryer basket, put the prepared ramekins, and cook for 12 minutes at about 300 degrees F/150 degrees C.
5. For two more minutes, add the remaining 4 fl. oz. of cheese and cook at 400 degrees F/205 degrees C.

Per serving:

- Kcal: 211; Carbs: 4g; Protein: 13.7g

18. Feta Stuffed Peppers with Broccoli

- Prep Time: 15 minutes | Cook time: 40 minutes | Serves: 2

INGREDIENTS

- 4 eggs
- 4 fl. oz cheddar cheese, grated
- 2 bell peppers cut in ½ and remove seeds.
- 2.5 ml garlic powder
- 15 ml dried thyme
- 59 ml feta cheese, crumbled
- 4 fl. oz broccoli, cooked
- 1 ml black pepper
- 2.5 ml salt

PREP

1. Your air fryer should be preheated to 325 degrees F, or 160 degrees C.
2. Place broccoli and feta inside the bell pepper halves.
3. In a suitable bowl, beat the egg with the seasoning before adding the feta, broccoli, and half of a black peppercorn. Bell peppers need to be chopped in half and fried in an air fryer basket for 35 to 40 minutes.
4. Cook until the grated cheddar cheese melts after being sprinkled on top.

Per serving:

- Kcal: 339; Carbs: 13g; 7g; Protein: 22.8g

19. Zucchini Muffins with Cinnamon

- Prep Time: 15 minutes | Cook time: 20 minutes **INGREDIENTS**
- 6 eggs
- four stevia drops
- 59 ml Swerve
- 8 fl. oz. of melted zucchini, 13 cup of coconut oil, and 177 ml. of shredded coconut flour
- a ml of ground nutmeg
- 15.0 ml of ground cinnamon
- 2.5 ml of baking soda

PREP

1. You should warm your air fryer to 325 degrees F, or 160 degrees C.
2. In a big bowl, combine all the ingredients for the recipe—aside from the zucchini—and toss well.
3. Add the zucchini and thoroughly stir.
4. Put the batter and the silicone muffin tins in the air fryer basket.
5. Muffins need 20 minutes to bake.

Per serving:

- Kcal: 111; Carbs: 8g; Net Carbs: 3.5g; Protein: 7.2g

20. Mushroom Frittata

- Prep Time: 15 minutes | Cook time: 6 minutes | Serves: 2

INGREDIENTS

- 3 lightly beaten eggs
- 10 ml of shredded cheddar cheese
- 2/fourths cup heavy cream
- 2 sliced mushrooms 1/4 small onion 1/4 diced bell pepper.
- Salt Black pepper

PREP

1. In a large bowl, combine the eggs, cream, salt, pepper, and vegetables.
2. Your air fryer should be preheated to 400 degrees F, or 205 degrees C.
3. The egg mixture should be added to the air fryer pan. The air fryer pan inside the air fryer basket should be cooked for 5 minutes.
4. The frittata should be cooked for a further minute after the cheese has been sprinkled on top.

Per serving:

- Kcal: 187; Carbs: 3g; Protein: 11.2g

21. Simple Cheddar-Omelet

- Prep Time: 15 minutes | Cook time: 10 minutes | Serves: 2

INGREDIENTS

- 4 eggs
- 60 ml cheddar, grated cheese
- ½ green onions, sliced
- ¼ tablespoon black pepper
- 15ml olive oil

PREP

1. Prepare each ingredient listed in the recipe.
2. Black pepper and the eggs are whisked together.

3. The air fryer should be preheated to roughly 350 degrees F (175 degrees C). Olive oil should be sprayed into the air fryer basket before adding the egg mixture and green onions.
4. For 8 to 10 minutes, air fry. Add some grated cheddar cheese on top.

Per serving:

- Kcal: 214; Carbs: 1g; Net Carbs: 0g; Protein: 14.7g

22. Strawberry Tarts

- Prep Time: 15 minutes | Cook time: 10 minutes | Serves: 6

INGREDIENTS

- 2 chilled pie crusts
- Strawberry preserves, 4 fl. oz.
- 15 ml of cornstarch
- frying-oil mist
- Low-fat vanilla yogurt, 4 fl. oz.
- 1 ounce of room temperature cream cheese
- 15 ml of sugar for confections
- sprinkles in rainbow colors for decoration

PREP

1. Place the pie crusts on a level surface.
2. Each piecrust should be divided into three rectangles using a knife or pizza cutter to make a total of six pieces. 3. In a suitable basin, mix the cornstarch and preserves. Completely combine.
3. The strawberry filling should be spread over the top half of each pie crust in a 15ml dollop.
4. To hide the contents, fold over the bottom of each piece.
5. Seal each tart by pushing around the edges with the back of a fork.
6. 350°F/175°C should be the temperature setting for your air fryer.
7. Spray cooking oil on the crisper plate of your air fryer after it has reached temperature.
8. As you work in batches, lightly mist the morning pastries with frying oil, then put them in a single layer in the basket.
9. The air fryer's temperature and time parameters should be 375 degrees Fahrenheit/190 degrees Celsius and 10 minutes, respectively.

10. Apply the same method to the other ingredients.
11. In a good bowl, mix the yogurt, cream cheese, and confectioners' sugar.
12. The breakfast tarts' tops can be decorated with sprinkles and icing.

Per serving:

- Kcal: 166; Carbs: 34.1g; Net Carbs: 1g; Protein: 2.3g

23. Italian Frittata with Feta Cheese

- Prep Time: 15 minutes | Cook time: 10 minutes | Serves: 6

INGREDIENTS

- 6 eggs
- 4 fl.oz of milk
- 4 ounces of chopped Italian sausage
- 3 cups of stemmed and roughly chopped kale
- 1 red deseeded and chopped bell pepper
- 4 fl. oz of a grated feta cheese
- 1 chopped zucchini
- 15ml of freshly chopped basil
- 15 ml of garlic powder
- 15 ml of onion powder
- 15 ml of salt
- 15 ml of black pepper

PREP

1. Set your air fryer to 180 degrees C or 360 degrees F before using. Use nonstick frying spray to oil the air fryer basket.
2. Italian sausage needs to be added to the basket and cooked in the air fryer for 5 minutes.
3. While doing that, add the remaining ingredients and carefully combine.
4. In your air fryer, add the prepared egg mixture to the pan and cook for 5 minutes.

Per serving:

- Kcal: 192; Carbs: 7g; Protein: 13g

24. Strawberry and Peach Toast

- 2-4 slices bread
- Strawberries, as needed
- 1 peach, corned and sliced
- 15 ml sugar
- Cooking spray
- 59 ml cream cheese
- 15 ml cinnamon

PREP

1. Prepare each ingredient listed in the recipe.
2. Olive oil should be sprayed on the bread's both sides.
3. Place in the air fryer basket that has been prepared, and cook for one minute on each side at roughly 375 degrees F/190 degrees C.
4. While preparing the other ingredients, slice the strawberries and peaches.
5. Thickly spread cream cheese on bread, decorate with strawberries and peaches, then, if you'd like, top with a sprinkling of cinnamon-almond mixture.

Per serving:

- Kcal: 97; Carbs: 10.1g; Net Carbs: 0g; Protein: 2.2g

25. Flavorful Scrambled Eggs with Chorizo

- 1 dash of Spanish paprika
- 1 dash of oregano
- 3 large eggs, beaten
- 15ml olive oil
- ½ zucchini, sliced
- ½ chorizo sausage, sliced

PREP

1. Prepare all the ingredients for the recipe.
2. Set your air fryer to 350 degrees F/175 degrees C. Salt and fry the zucchini for two to three minutes in olive oil.
3. Cook the zucchini and chorizo together for an additional 5 to 6 minutes.
4. Return the basket to the air fryer for 5 minutes after filling with the egg mixture, remove it, and stir it every minute until it is cooked...

Per serving:

- Kcal: 186; Carbs: 2g; Net Carbs: 0.5g; Protein: 10.7g

26. Spinach Frittata with Mozzarella

- 3 eggs
- 8 fl.oz spinach, chopped.
- 1 small onion, minced
- 30 ml mozzarella cheese, grated.
- Black pepper
- Salt

PREP

1. 350°F/175°C should be the temperature setting for your air fryer. In the basket of the air fryer, spray cooking spray.
2. In a large bowl, whisk eggs with remaining ingredients until well combined.
3. Before adding the prepared egg mixture to the pan, place the pan in the heated air fryer basket. Cook the frittata for 8 minutes, or until set. After serving, indulge.

Per serving:

- Kcal: 384; Carbs: 10.7g; Protein: 34.3g

27. Awesome Everything Bagels

- 4 fl. oz self-rising flour
- 4 fl. oz plain Greek yogurt
- 1 egg
- 15ml water
- 20 ml everything bagel spice mix
- Cooking oil spray
- 15ml butter, melted.

PREP

1. The flour and yogurt should be combined in a good bowl and stirred with a wooden spoon until a sticky dough develops.
2. Roll the dough into a ball and transfer it to a lightly dusted work surface.
3. The dough should be divided into two parts and rolled into logs. Pinch the ends of each log together as you mold them into bagel shapes.
4. Whisk the egg and water in a good bowl. On the bagels, use egg wash.
5. Each bagel should receive 10 ml of the spice mixture, which you should gently press into the dough.
6. Spray cooking spray onto the crisper plate after your air fryer equipment has reached the preheating stage.
7. Place the bagels in the basket after buttering them and placing them there.
8. Pre-heat your air fryer to 330 degrees F/165 degrees C, then cook for 10 minutes.
9. The bagels should have a light golden outside after cooking is done. 10. Serve hot.

Per serving:

- Kcal 224; Carbs: 25g;16g; Protein: 10.6g

28. Sweet Berry Muffins

- 14 fl.ozs 15ml all-purpose flour
- 59 ml granulated sugar
- 30 mls light brown sugar
- 10 ml baking powder
- 2 eggs
- 8 fl .oz whole milk
- 4 fl.oz safflower oil
- 8 fl.oz mixed fresh berries

PREP

1. 14 fl. oz. of flour, granulated sugar, brown sugar, and baking powder should be thoroughly combined in a good basin.
2. Whisk the eggs, milk, and oil together in a suitable bowl.
3. Just combine the dry components with the prepared egg mixture.
4. The leftover 15ml of flour should be combined with the mixed berries in a another bowl to coat them. Incorporate the berries slowly into the batter.
5. To create 8 cups, fold the 16 foil muffin liners together.
6. Place 4 cups into the basket of your air fryer after it has finished heating up, and fill each one 3/4 full with the batter.
7. Set your air fryer to 315 degrees F/155 degrees C and cook for 17 minutes. For the remaining cups, repeat the cooking procedures.

Per serving:

- Kcal: 198; Carbs: 22g; Protein: 3.5g

29. Creamy Soufflés

- 6 large eggs, separated.
- 177 ml heavy cream
- 1 ml cayenne pepper
- 2.5 ml xanthan gum
- 2.5 ml black pepper
- 1 ml cream of tartar
- 30 mls chives, chopped.
- 12 fl .oz cheddar cheese, shredded.
- 15 ml salt

PREP

1. Pre-heat your air fryer to 325 degrees F or 160 degrees C.
2. Cooking spray ought to be used on eight ramekins. Place aside.
3. Almond flour, xanthan gum, salt, cayenne pepper, and black pepper should all be combined in an appropriate basin.
4. Heavy cream should be added gradually; blend.
5. Add the cheese, chives, and egg yolks and mix thoroughly.
6. Egg whites and cream of tartar should be combined in a good bowl, then beaten until stiff peaks form.
7. Until mixed, fold the egg white mixture into the dry almond flour mixture.
8. Fill the ramekins with the prepared mixture. Divide the ramekins into groups.
9. Put the air fryer basket with the first batch of ramekins inside.
10. 20-minute soufflé cooking time.

Per serving:

- Kcal: 207; Carbs: 1g; Protein: 12g

30. Egg Soufflé with Mushroom and Broccoli

- 4 large eggs
- 15 ml onion powder
- 15 ml garlic powder
- 15 ml red pepper, crushed.
- 4 fl. oz broccoli florets, chopped.
- 4 fl. oz mushrooms, chopped.

PREP

1. 4 ramekins should be coated with cooking spray before being set aside.
2. In a sturdy basin, whisk eggs with red pepper flakes, onion powder, and garlic powder.
3. Add the broccoli and mushrooms and stir well.
4. The egg mixture should be placed inside the ramekins before placing them in the air fryer basket.
5. Cook at 175 degrees Celsius/nearly 350 degrees Fahrenheit for around 15 minutes. If the soufflé isn't cooked, cook it for an extra five minutes.

Per serving:

- Kcal: 91; Carbs: 4.7g; Protein: 7.4g

Meat Recipes

31. Kansas City's Baby Back Rib Recipe

- Servings: 2
- Prep & Cooking Time: 50 Minutes

Ingredients:

- 2 fl.oz white wine vinegar
- 2 fl.oz molasses
- 1 ml. cayenne pepper
- 8 fl.oz ketchup
- 15 ml. brown sugar
- 15 ml. liquid smoke seasoning, hickory
- 15 ml. Worcestershire sauce
- 5 ml. dry mustard
- 1-lb. pork ribs, small
- 2 cloves of garlic
- Salt & pepper to taste

Directions:

1. Combine all the ingredients in a Ziploc bag, then chill for at least two hours.
2. 390 °F should be the air fryer's temperature.
3. Place the grill pan attachment on the air fryer.
4. Per batch, grill the meat for 25 minutes.
5. Midway during the cooking process, turn the meat over.
6. Pour the marinade into a pot, then cook it until the sauce is thick.
7. Before serving, brush the meat with glaze.

32. Top Round Roast With Herbs Blend

- Servings: 10
- Prep & Cooking Time: 1 Hour

Ingredients:

- 5 ml. dry mustard
- 30 ml. dried rosemary
- 3 tbsps. olive oil
- 4 lbs. beef top round roast
- 60 ml. dried oregano
- 60 ml. dried oregano
- Salt & pepper to taste

Directions:

1. Give the air fryer five minutes to warm up.
2. In a baking dish that will fit in the air fryer, combine all the ingredients.
3. Cook the food for an hour at 50°F in the air fryer.

33. Pork In Garlic Sauce

- Servings: 4
- Prep & Cooking Time: 25 Minutes

Ingredients:

- Sliced pork tenderloin weighing 1 lb.
- a dash of black pepper and salt
- Melted butter, 60 ml.
- minced garlic, 30 ml.
- sweet paprika, 5 ml.

Directions:

1. Pre-heat a skillet that will fit an air fryer with the butter over medium heat, excluding the pork medallions. Stir everything together, then add everything and cook for 4-5 minutes.
2. In an air fryer, the pork should be added, combined, and fried for 20 minutes at 380°F.
3. The combination should be divided among plates with a side salad.

34. Peanut Sauce With Flavorsome Pork Chops

- Servings: 4
- Prep & Cooking Time: 12 Minutes

Ingredients:

- Pork chops weighing 1 lb, cut into 1-inch cubes
- 1 minced shallot finely
- Peanuts, ground, 6 fl. oz.
- Coconut milk, 6 fl. oz.
- Regarding pork:
- 5 ml of freshly minced ginger.
- 1 minced garlic clove.
- 2 tablespoons soy sauce
- Olive oil, 15 ml
- 5 milliliters of spicy sauce

For Peanut Sauce:

- Olive oil, 15 ml
- 1 minced garlic clove.
- Ground coriander, 5 ml.
- Olive oil, 15 ml
- 5 milliliters of spicy sauce

Directions:

1. Heat the air fryer to 390°F while greasing a basket.
2. In a bowl, combine all the ingredients for the pork; leave it alone for about five minutes.
3. After placing the chops in the air fryer basket, they should be cooked for 12 minutes, flipping once.
4. Before incorporating the shallot and garlic into the peanut sauce, preheat the olive oil in a medium saucepan.
5. After three minutes of sautéing, add the coriander.
6. Add the remaining ingredients when the sautéing has lasted about a minute.
7. After cooking the pork chops for about 5 minutes, place them on a serving dish.

35. Loin Chops With Za'atar Lamb

- Servings: 4

Ingredients:

- 8 lamb loin chops (3 1/2 ounces), trimmed 3 garlic cloves, and 15 ml. fresh lemon juice
- Olive oil, 5 ml; 15 ml. Za'ataro
- To taste, add black pepper and salt.

Directions:

1. Heat the air fryer to 400 degrees and grease the air fryer basket.
2. Combine the oil, garlic, lemon juice, Za'atar, salt, and black pepper in a big bowl.
3. After generously coating the chops with the herb mixture, place them in the air fryer basket.
4. The lamb chops should be cooked for approximately 15 minutes, turning them over twice, and then serving them hot.

36. Short Loin Steak With Grilled Mayo

- Prep & Cooking Time: 20 Minutes

Ingredients:

- 8 ounces of mayonnaise
- 2 tablespoons of finely minced fresh rosemary, 15 ml. Sauce worcestershire
- to taste, sea salt
- Ground black pepper, half a teaspoon
- Smoked paprika, 5 ml.
- minced garlic, 5 ml.
- 1.25 pounds of short loin steak

Directions:

1. Salt, pepper, paprika, garlic, rosemary, Worcestershire sauce, and mayonnaise; blend thoroughly.
2. Apply the mayonnaise mixture on the steak now and brush it on both sides. Onto the grill pan goes the steak.

3. Grill for eight minutes at 400°F in the preheated air fryer. Grill the steaks for an additional 7 minutes on the other side.
4. Use a meat thermometer to check the doneness.
5. Enjoy warm servings!

37. Potatoes With Pork Loin

- Prep & Cooking Time: 25 Minutes

Ingredients:

- a 2-pound pork loin
- 3 large red potatoes, minced, 5 ml. fresh parsley, 3 tbsp. olive oil, divided
- if needed, salt and freshly ground black pepper
- Garlic powder, 2.5 ml
- 2.5 ml of crushed red pepper flakes

Directions:

1. Heat the air fryer to 325°F and grease an air fryer pan.
2. The pork loin should be evenly coated with 1 1/30 ml of olive oil, parsley, salt, and black pepper.
3. Add the potatoes, remaining oil, salt, pepper, garlic powder, and red pepper flakes to a bowl.
4. Potato pieces should be placed around the pork loin's edges in the air fryer basket.
5. After about 2 minutes of cooking, serve in a bowl.
6. Slices of the chosen thickness should be placed next to the potatoes.

38. Dill Pickles With Smoked Brisket

- Prep & Cooking Time: 1 Hour

Ingredients:

- 1.0 milliliter of liquid smoke
- 8 ounces of dill pickles
- 3 pounds of flat-cut brisket.
- Pepper and salt to taste

Directions:

1. Set the air fryer to 390°F before use.
2. Liquid smoke, salt, and pepper are used to season the brisket before placing it on the grill pan and cooking it in batches for about 30 minutes each.
3. For even grilling, turn the meat halfway through cooking.
4. Dill pickles are recommended.

39. Worcester Meatloaf

- Prep & Cooking Time: 35 Minutes

Ingredients:

- 1 large onion, chopped after peeling.
- 5 ml of beef mince in 2 kg. Wroclaw sauce
- 15 ml of 3 tbsp. tomato ketchup. 15 ml of oregano and 15 ml of basil. 15 ml of mixed herbs. welcoming breadcrumbs
- pepper and salt to taste

Directions:

1. Mix the mince thoroughly with the herbs, Worcester sauce, onion, and tomato ketchup in a large basin.
2. Add the breadcrumbs, then whisk once more.
3. Place the mixture in a small dish and air fried it for 25 minutes at 380°F.

40. Wine Marinated Flank Steak

- Servings: 4

Ingredients:

- 1.5 lbs. of flank steak
- 4-ounces of red wine
- 4 ounces of white wine vinegar
- Soy sauce, 30 ml
- Salt, as desired
- Ground black pepper, 2.5 ml
- 2.5 ml of crushed red pepper flakes
- Basil, dried, 2.5 ml.
- Thyme, 5 ml.

Directions:

1. Before using the air fryer, heat it up to 400°F.
2. All the ingredients should be combined in a large porcelain bowl. Cover it and marinate it for three hours in your refrigerator.
3. Place the flank steak in the greased, air fryer basket covered with nonstick cooking oil.
4. In the hot air fryer, cook for 12 minutes, flipping the food over halfway through. Happy eating!

41. Pork Roulade

- Servings: 2

Ingredients:

- 2 chops of pork
- German mustard, 5 ml.
- 5 ml. diced chives
- 1 diced pickled cucumber
- Almond butter, 5 ml.
- Ground black pepper, 2.5 ml
- Olive oil, 5 ml

Directions:

1. Beat the pork chops gently with the help of the kitchen hammer and place them on the chopping board overlap.
2. Then rub the meat with ground black pepper and German mustard.
3. Top it with chives, diced pickled cucumber, and almond butter.
4. Roll the meat into the roulade and secure it with the kitchen thread.
5. Then sprinkle the roulade with olive oil.
6. Preheat the air fryer to 390°F.
7. Put the roulade in the air fryer and cook it for 15 minutes.
8. Slice the cooked roulade.

42. Old-Fashioned Beef Burgers

- Servings: 6

Ingredients:

- 2 lbs. ground beef
- 12 cheddar cheese slices
- 12 dinner rolls
- 6 tbsps. tomato ketchup
- Salt & black pepper, to taste

Directions:

1. Grease an air fryer basket and preheat the air fryer to 390°F.
2. In a bowl, combine the meat, salt, and black pepper.
3. From the beef mixture, form tiny, equal-sized patties, and place half of them in the air fryer basket.
4. After 12 minutes of cooking, add 1 slice of cheese to each burger.
5. Spread ketchup on the patties before placing them between rolls.
6. Repeat the process with the remaining batch, then serve warm.

43. Beef Jerky

- Servings: 3

Ingredients:

- 1 lb. bottom round beef, cut into slim strips
- Dark brown sugar, 4 fl. oz.
- 4 ounces of soy sauce
- Worcestershire sauce, 2 fluid ounces
- 15 milliliters of hot sauce
- Hickory liquid smoke in 15 ml
- Garlic powder, 5 ml.
- 0.5 ml of onion powder
- Cayenne pepper, 5 ml
- Smoked paprika, 2.5 ml.
- Ground black pepper, 2.5 ml

Directions:

1. Air fryer should be preheated to 0°F and basket should be greased.
2. Combine the sauces, brown sugar, liquid smoke, and spices in a bowl.
3. This marinade should be generously applied to the beef strips before leaving it to marinate overnight.
4. Put half of the beef strips in the air fryer basket in a single layer.
5. The frying rack should be covered with the remaining meat strips.
6. Serve the food after cooking for about an hour.

44. Vegetables With Hearty Beef Cubes

- Servings: 4

Ingredients:

- 30 ml. olive oil and 1 lb. diced top round steak
- White wine vinegar in 15 ml
- 0.5 ml of fine sea salt
- Ground black pepper, 2.5 ml
- Shallot powder, 5 ml
- Smoked cayenne pepper, 3/4 teaspoon
- Garlic powder, 2.5 ml
- Cumin seed, 1 milliliter
- 1/4 pound of floretized broccoli
- Sliced mushrooms, 1/4 pound, and 5 cc of dried basil
- Celery seeds, 5 ml

Directions:

1. The beef should first be marinated in a mixture of olive oil, vinegar, salt, black pepper, cumin, shallot powder, and cayenne pepper. Then, leave it for at least three hours after giving it a good toss to coat.
2. The air fryer cooking basket should contain beef cubes, which should be fried for 1 minute at 365°F. When the cubes are finished, turn off the machine, check to make sure they are, and then put them in a bowl.
3. After cleaning the cooking basket, add the celery, basil seeds, and veggies and toss to coat.
4. The vegetables should be cooked for 5 to 6 minutes, or until they are well heated, in an oven set at 400 degrees Fahrenheit.
5. Serve with the meat chunks you saved. Good appetite!

45. Buttered Strip Loin Steak

- Servings: 2

Ingredients:

- two (7-ounce) strip steaks
- 1 1/30 ml. softened butter
- to taste, softened.ck pepper

Directions:

1. Heat the air fryer to 390°F while greasing a basket.
2. After thoroughly seasoning the meat with salt and pepper, butter should be used.
3. Put the steak in the air fryer basket and cook it for about 12 minutes, flipping it once.
4. Before serving, slice the meat into serving-size pieces.

46. Buttered Garlic-Celery With Roast Beef

- Servings: 8

Ingredients:

- 1 crushed and peeled bulb of garlic
- 15.0 ml of butter
- Two medium onions, minced, and two pounds of topside beef
- 2 cut celery sticks, 3 tablespoons of olive oil
- 2 fl oz of your preferred fresh herbs
- Pepper and salt to taste

Directions:

1. Give the air fryer five minutes to warm up.
2. Stir well after adding all the ingredients to the air fryer pan.
3. Bake the dish for an hour at 300°F in the air fryer.

47. Smoked Pork

- Servings: 5

Ingredients:

- 1-lb. pork shoulder
- 15 ml. liquid smoke
- 15 ml. olive oil
- 5 ml. salt

Directions:

1. Before using, preheat the air fryer to 390°F.
2. Combine the liquid smoke, salt, and olive oil in a small bowl. The liquid smoke mixture should then be carefully brushed over the pork shoulder on both sides.
3. Make little amounts of the beef cuts. In the air fryer basket, the pork shoulder should be cooked for 10 minutes.
4. On the other side, cook the meat for a further 10 minutes. Ten to fifteen minutes should be allowed for the cooked pork shoulder to rest.
5. You can shred it with the aid of two forks.

48. Cumin Lamb Kebabs, Sichuan And Caraway

- Servings: 3

Ingredients:

- Lamb shoulder weighing 1 1/2 pounds, with the bones removed and 15 ml of pieces. peppercorns from Sichuan
- 5 ml sugar, 30 ml roasted cumin seeds, 30 ml toasted caraway seeds, and 30 ml. flakes of crushed red pepper
- Pepper and salt to taste

Directions:

1. Put all the ingredients in a bowl, and marinate the meat in the refrigerator for 30 minutes.
2. the air fryer to 390°F before using.
3. Place each batch of meat on the grill for 15 minutes.
4. To ensure even cooking, flip the meat every 8 minutes.

49. Hot Paprika Beef

- Servings: 4

Ingredients:

- 15 ml. hot paprika
- 4 beef steaks
- Salt & black pepper to the taste
- 15 ml. butter, melted

Directions:

1. The steaks should be placed in the basket of your air fryer and cooked at 390°F for 15 minutes on each side after being thoroughly mixed with the remaining ingredients in a bowl.
2. Place the steaks on individual dishes and accompany with a side salad.

50. Hot Bacon Bites

- Servings: 4

Ingredients:

- 4 bacon strips, cut into small pieces
- 4 fl. oz pork rinds, crushed
- 2 fl .oz hot sauce

Directions:

1. Add some bacon to the bowl.
2. Stir thoroughly after adding spicy sauce.
3. Once the bacon bits are thoroughly coated, add the crumbled pig rinds and stir.
4. Place the bacon chunks in the air fryer basket and cook for 10 minutes at 350°F.
5. Enjoy after serving.

51. Beef Schnitzel

- Servings: 1

Ingredients:

- 1 egg
- a single thin beef schnitzel
- 3 tablespoons of fine bread crumbs
- Olive oil, 30 ml
- 1 teaspoon of roughly minced parsley 1/2 wedge of lemon

Directions:

1. Ahead of time, preheat your air fryer to 360°F.
2. In a mixing bowl, combine the bread crumbs, salt, and olive oil to form a loose, crumbly mixture.
3. The egg should be whisked.
4. After bathing the schnitzel in the egg, be sure to completely cover it with breadcrumbs.
5. The air fryer should be used to cook the schnitzel for 12 to 14 minutes. Add the lemon wedges and parsley to the schnitzel before serving.

52. Sage Sauce Recipe With Pork Chops

- Servings: 2

Ingredients:

- 2 chops of pork
- 1 sliced shallot
- 1 handful of minced sage
- To taste, add black pepper and salt.
- Olive oil, 15 ml
- 30 ml of butter
- Lemon juice, 5 ml.

Directions:

1. Cooking pork in an air fryer at 370 °F for 20 minutes, flipping the pieces over halfway through, requires seasoning with salt and pepper to taste.

2. Melt the butter in a pan over medium heat in the interim. The shallot should be added and cooked for a few minutes.
3. Sage and lemon juice are added; the mixture is thoroughly mixed before the heat is turned off.
4. Pork chops should be divided among plates, then served with sage sauce.

53. Meatball Sausage

- Servings: 4

Ingredients:

- 31/2-ounce sausage, casing removed
- 1/2 medium onion, minced finely
- 5 ml. fresh sage, minced finely
- 3 tbsps. Italian breadcrumbs
- 2.5 ml. garlic, minced
- Salt & black pepper, to taste

Directions:

1. Heat the air fryer to 355°F after greasing the basket.
2. Completely combine all the ingredients in a bowl.
3. Make equal-sized balls from the mixture, and then put the balls in the air fryer's basket.
4. 15 minutes should be added to the cooking time before serving warm.

54. Ghee Mushroom With Beef Mix

- Servings: 4
- Prep & Cooking Time: 25 Minutes

Ingredients:

- 4 beef steaks
- 15 ml. olive oil
- A pinch of salt and black pepper
- 30 mls. ghee, melted
- melted.. cloves, minced minced.ps wild mushrooms, sliced
- 15 ml. parsley, minced.

Directions:

1. The steaks should be cooked in an air fryer-compatible skillet that has been prepared with oil over medium-high heat for 2 minutes on each side.
2. The additional ingredients must be included, combined, and air-fried for 20 minutes at 380°F.
3. Serve after distributing among plates.

55. Cumin-Paprika With Beef Brisket

- Servings: 12

Ingredients:

- Cayenne pepper, 1 milliliter
- Paprika, 1 1/30 ml.
- Garlic powder, 5 ml.
- 0.5 ml of ground cumin
- 0.5 ml of onion powder
- 30 milliliters each of dry mustard and powdered black pepper
- Salt, 30 ml.
- five-pound brisket roast
- 5 tablespoons olive oil

Directions:

1. The air fryer should be set to 350°F for frying.
2. In a Ziploc bag, combine all the ingredients, and chill for at least two hours.
3. Place the meat in an air fryer-compatible baking dish.
4. Place there and cook for two hours in the air fryer.

Fish and Seafood Recipes

56. Asian Swordfish

- 4 swordfish steaks, weighing 113 grams each.
- Sesame oil, roasted, 2.5 ml
- One jalapeno pepper, minced finely.
- 15ml of freshly grated ginger and two grated garlic cloves
- Chinese five-spice powder, 2.5 ml
- freshly ground black pepper, 1/8 teaspoon
- Freshly squeezed lemon juice, 30 milliliters

preparation

1. On a work surface, arrange the swordfish steaks and sprinkle with sesame oil.
2. Combine the jalapeno, garlic, ginger, five-spice powder, pepper, and lemon juice in a small bowl. Ten minutes after applying this mixture to the fish, set it aside.
3. When the swordfish reaches an internal temperature of at least 140°F (60°C) on a meat thermometer, roast it in the air fryer at 380°F (193°C) for 6 to 11 minutes. Serve right away.

57. Tilapia Sandwiches with Tartar Sauce

- MAYO, 177 milliliters
- Dry minced onion, 30 milliliters
- 1 spear of dill pickles, coarsely chopped
- 10% pickle juice
- A milliliter of salt
- freshly ground black pepper, 1/8 teaspoon
- a third cup of all-purpose flour
- 1 gently beaten egg
- Panko bread crumbs 1177 ml
- 1 teaspoon lemon pepper
- 4 (6-ounce/170-g) fillets of tilapia
- Olive oil aerosol
- four hoagies
- 4 leaves of butter lettuce

Preparation

1. Mayonnaise, pickle, dried onion, pickle juice, salt, and pepper should all be combined in a small bowl to form the tartar sauce. When preparing the seafood, keep refrigerated.
2. The flour should be thrown onto a plate and left there.
3. the beaten egg in a medium-sized shallow bowl.
4. On a different plate, combine the panko and lemon pepper.
5. Place the crisper plate inside the basket and the basket inside the unit. To preheat the appliance, choose AIR FRY, set the temperature to 400°F (204°C), and set the timer for 3 minutes. Select START/STOP to begin.
6. The best way to coat tilapia fillets is to dredge them in a mixture of flour, egg, and panko.
7. After the device has heated up, spray the crisper plate with olive oil, then place a parchment paper liner within the basket. Place the prepared fillets on the lining in a single layer. lightly mist the fillets with olive oil.
8. Set the temperature and timings to 400°F (204°C) after selecting AIR FRY. Select START/STOP to begin.
9. After eight minutes, take out the basket, carefully turn the fillets, and then spray them with more olive oil. Re-insert the basket to resume cooking.
10. When the fillets have completed frying, they should be golden and crispy, and a food thermometer should read 145°F (63°C). Before being served, each grilled fillet needs to be stuffed onto a hoagie sandwich with lettuce and tartar sauce.

58. Quick Shrimp Skewers

- 4 pounds (1.8 kg) of peeled shrimp
- 15 ml dried thyme
- apple cider vinegar and 15ml of avocado oil

Preparation

1. Mix the shrimps with dried rosemary, avocado oil, and apple cider vinegar.
2. Then sting the shrimps into skewers and put in the air fryer.
3. Cook the shrimps at 400ºF (204ºC) for 5 minutes.

59. Crispy Fish Sticks

- 1 ounce (28 g) pork rinds, finely ground
- 59 ml blanched finely ground almond flour
- 2.5 ml Old Bay seasoning
- 15ml coconut oil
- 1 large egg
- 1 pound (454 g) cod fillet, cut into ¾-inch strips

Preparation

1. Mix together in a sizable bowl the ground pork rinds, almond flour, Old Bay flavor, and coconut oil. Whisk the egg in a medium basin.
2. Each fish stick should be dipped into the egg, carefully pressed into the flour mixture, and coated as completely and uniformly as possible. Put the air fryer basket with the fish sticks inside.
3. Turn up the heat to 400°F (204°C), then air fried the food for 10 minutes, or until golden. 4. Serve right away.

60. Mustard-Crusted Fish Fillets

- Low-sodium yellow mustard, 5 tablespoons
- Lemon juice, freshly squeezed, 15 ml
- 4 sole fillets (99 g, or 312 ounces).
- 2.5 mg of dried thyme
- 2.5 ml of dried marjoram
- freshly ground black pepper, 1/8 teaspoon
- 1 crumbled slice of low-sodium whole-wheat bread
- 1/10 milliliter of olive oil

Preparation

1. In a small bowl, mix the lemon juice and mustard. Distribute this equally over the fillets. Place them in the air fryer's basket.
2. In a different tiny bowl, mix the thyme, marjoram, pepper, bread crumbs, and olive oil. Put together through merging.
3. Each salmon fillet should have the spice mixture gently but firmly placed onto it. 4. Bake for 8 to 11 minutes, or until the topping is browned and crisp and a meat thermometer reads at least 145°F (63°C) for the internal temperature of the fish. Serve immediately.

61. Rockfish with Avocado Cream

- Fish Fillets:
- 17.5 mls balsamic vinegar
- 4 fl. oz vegetable broth
- 2.5 ml shallot powder
- 15ml coconut aminos
- 4 Rockfish fillets
- 15 ml ground black pepper
- 17.5 mls olive oil
- Fine sea salt, to taste
- 2.5 ml garlic powder
- Avocado Cream:
- 30 mls Greek-style yogurt
- 1 clove garlic peeled and minced.
- 15 ml ground black pepper
- 7.5 ml olive oil
- 80 ml vegetable broth
- 1 avocado
- 2.5 ml lime juice
- 2.5 ml fine sea salt

Preparation

1. After being rinsed in a bowl, the fillets should be dried with several paper towels. Add every seasoning. Combine the other ingredients for the fish fillets in a separate bowl.
2. The fish fillets should be added, covered, and marinated in the refrigerator for at least three hours.
3. The air fryer should then be set to 325°F (163°C). In the grill basket of an air fryer, cook marinated rockfish fillets for nine minutes.
4. While you wait, make the avocado sauce by blending all the ingredients in a normal or immersion blender. Top the rockfish fillets with the avocado sauce and serve. Enjoy!

62. Cayenne Flounder Cutlets

- 1 egg, 8 fl. oz. grated Pecorino Romano cheese with a dash of white pepper and sea salt, to taste
- Cayenne pepper, 2.5 milliliters
- 15 ml of flaked dried parsley
- Flake fillets, two

Preparation

1. Whisk the egg until foamy to create a breading station.
2. In a dish, the fillets should be rinsed and dried with some paper towels. Incorporate each seasoning. The additional ingredients for the fish fillets should be combined in a separate bowl.
3. The fish fillets should be added, covered, and marinated for at least three hours in the refrigerator.
4. Following that, preheat the air fryer to 325°F (163°C). Cook marinated rockfish fillets in the grill basket of an air fryer for nine minutes.
5. Use a conventional or immersion blender to puree the ingredients for the avocado sauce while you wait. With the avocado sauce on top, serve the rockfish fillets. Enjoy!

63. Shrimp Scampi

- 12 stick of salted butter or ghee, 60 ml.
- 15 milliliters of lemon juice
- 15ml minced garlic
- Red pepper flakes in 10 ml
- Peeled and deveined 21 to 25 count shrimp weighing 1 pound (454 g)
- 30 ml of dry white wine or chicken broth
- 15 ml dried basil, or 30 mls of fresh basil chopped with additional for sprinkling
- 15 ml of fresh chopped chives or 15 ml of dried

Preparation

1. A baking pan should be put in the air fryer basket. For eight minutes, set the air fryer to 325°F (163°C) (this will preheat the pan so the butter will melt faster).
2. Butter, lemon juice, garlic, and red pepper flakes should be added after carefully removing the pan from the fryer. Reintroduce the pan to the fryer.
3. Once the butter has melted, cook for an additional two minutes while stirring. (Don't omit this step; it gives the butter its flavorful infusion of garlic, which is what makes everything taste so nice.) 4. Carefully take the pan out of the fryer, then add the stock, basil, and chives. Then add the shrimp. Gently blend the ingredients by stirring just until incorporated.
4. After five minutes, add the pan back to the air fryer and cook while stirring.
5. Stir the shrimp mixture well before giving it a minute to rest on a wire rack. (This helps prevent overcooking and rubbery shrimp by allowing the shrimp to cook in the residual heat.)
6. Repeat the stirring, top with extra finely chopped fresh basil, and serve.

64. Sole and Asparagus Bundles

- 8 ounces (227 g) of trimmed asparagus
- Extra virgin olive oil, 15 ml, divided
- To taste, add salt and pepper.
- 4 skinless sole or flounder fillets, each measuring 3 ounces (85 grams).
- 60 ml of softened unsalted butter
- 15ml of fresh tarragon, cut from one small shallot,
- Vegetable oil spray with 1 ml of lemon juice and 2.5 ml of zest

Preparation

1. Set the air fryer's thermostat to 300°F (149°C).
2. In a bowl, toss the asparagus with 2.5 ml oil, a pinch of salt, and a pinch of pepper. For about 3 minutes, cover and microwave the spinach until it is bright green and just soft, stirring halfway through. Uncover it and leave it alone to cool a little.
3. Fold 1 long sheet of aluminum foil into a 4 inch-wide sling to fit the air fryer basket. Lay a layer of foil across the basket widthwise, pressing it into the bottom and up the sides. If necessary, fold any extra foil so that the edges are flush with the top of the basket. Spray foil and the basket with vegetable oil spray sparingly.
4. With paper towels, pat the sole dry before seasoning it with salt and pepper. Place fillets on chopping board, skin side up, with thicker ends closest to you. Each fillet should have asparagus placed evenly across the base. Next, tightly roll the fillets away from you to enclose the asparagus in neat bundles.
5. Bundles are placed seam side down on a sling in the prepared basket after being uniformly rubbed with the remaining 2.5 cc oil. Bake for 14 to 18 minutes, rotating the bundles with a sling halfway through cooking, or until the asparagus is tender and the sole easily flakes apart when lightly poked with a paring knife.
6. In a bowl, mix the butter, shallot, tarragon, and lemon juice. Carefully remove the sole bundles from the air fryer and place them on individual plates using a sling. Add the butter mixture evenly on top, then plate.

65. Tuna-Stuffed Quinoa Patties

- 340 g (12 oz) of quinoa
- 4 crustless slices of white bread
- 4 ounces of milk
- 3 eggs
- ten ounces (283 g) tuna in olive oil, drained, with two to three lemons
- To taste, add kosher salt and pepper.
- Panko breadcrumbs, 159 ml
- Vegetable oil for use as a spray
- serving slices of lemon

Preparation

1. Rinse the quinoa in a fine-mesh sieve until the water is crystal clear. Boiling water should occur after adding 4 cups of salt. Add the quinoa, reduce the heat to low, and cover. For 15 to 20 minutes, or until most of the water has been absorbed and the quinoa is tender, cook the quinoa, covered. Drain, then let the mixture to warm up. In the interim, milk should be soaked into bread.
2. The drained quinoa, sopped bread, and 2 of the eggs should all be combined in a large bowl. Stir thoroughly. In a medium bowl, combine the tuna, the last egg, and the juice and zest of 1 lemon. To taste, add salt and pepper. The panko should be dispersed on a dish.
3. Make patties out of the quinoa mixture using about 4 fl. oz. A heaping tablespoon of the tuna combination should be placed in the center of the quinoa to seal the quinoa around the tuna. The patties should be gently flattened to create an oval croquette. Place the croquette there and cover both sides with panko. Use the remaining quinoa and tuna to continue.
4. To prevent the basket from sticking, pre-heat the air fryer to 400°F (204°C). Carefully place four or five croquettes in the basket without crowding them. Spray some oil on the croquettes' tops. After 8 minutes in the air fryer, the top ought to be crispy and browned. Gently flip the croquettes over and spray the opposite side with oil. Air-fry the second side for an additional 7 minutes, or until it is golden and crispy. Repeat with the remaining croquettes.
5. Lots of lemon wedges should be provided for spritzing with warm croquetas.

66. Country Shrimp

- 1 pound (454 g) of large, deveined shrimp with the tails on and 1 pound (454 g) of thickly sliced smoked turkey sausage
- 2 quartered cobs of corn
- 1 zucchini, diced up into small pieces.
- one red bell pepper, chopped
- Old Bay seasoning in 15 ml
- Olive oil, 30 ml
- frying oil

Preparation

1. The temperature should be 400°F (204°C) on the air fryer. Use cooking spray to lightly spritz the air fryer basket.
2. In a big bowl, combine the shrimp, turkey sausage, corn, zucchini, bell pepper, and Old Bay seasoning. Toss to blend. Add the olive oil and continue tossing until everything is evenly covered.
3. The mixture needs to be dispersed equally throughout the air fryer basket. Batches must be used for cooking.
4. During the 15 to 20 minutes of air frying, shake the basket every five minutes to achieve equal cooking.
5. Serve immediately.

67. Steamed Cod with Garlic and Swiss Chard

- Salt, 15 ml.
- 2.4 ml dried oregano
- 2.5 mg of dried thyme
- 2.5 mg of garlic powder
- 4 fillets of cod
- 12 of a finely sliced white onion
- 12 fl .oz Swiss chard that has been washed, stemmed, and shredded
- Olive oil, 59 ml
- 1 quartered lemon

Preparation

1. Achieve a 380°F (193°C) air fryer temperature.
2. Combine the salt, oregano, thyme, and garlic powder in a small bowl.
3. Four sheets of aluminum foil, each big enough to hold a fish fillet and a quarter of the veggies, should be torn off.
4. Each foil sheet should have a cod fillet in the center. Sprinkle the spice mixture over the fish on all sides.
5. Place a quarter of the onion slices and 4 fl. oz. of Swiss chard in each foil packet before covering the contents with 15 ml of olive oil and 14 of a lemon.
6. The foil packages should be placed into the air fryer basket after being folded and sealed on all sides. For 12 minutes, steam.
7. To prevent a steam burn, take each package out of the basket and open it slowly.

68. Cucumber and Salmon Salad

- 1 pound (454 g) of salmon fillet, rinsed and drained, 17.5 ml of olive oil, 15 ml of sherry vinegar, and 15 ml of capers.
- 1 thinly sliced seedless cucumber, 1/4 sliced Vidalia onion, and 30 milliliters of freshly chopped parsley
- To taste, add salt and freshly ground black pepper.

Preparation

1. The temperature should be 400°F (204°C) on the air fryer.
2. Sparingly drizzle the salmon with 7.5 cc of the olive oil. Place skin-side down in the air fryer basket and air fry for 8 to 10 minutes, or until the fish is opaque and flakes easily with a fork. Transfer the salmon to a plate once it has cooled to room temperature. By delicately removing the skin from the fish and flaking it into bite-sized pieces.
3. In a small bowl, thoroughly combine the vinegar and the 15ml of remaining olive oil. Add flakes of fish, capers, cucumber, onion, and parsley. To taste, add salt and freshly ground black pepper. Toss gently to coat. You can cover and chill for up to four hours before serving.

69. Dukkah-Crusted Halibut

Dukkah:

- Coriander seeds, 15 ml
- Sesame seeds, 15 ml
- Cumin seeds in 12.5 ml
- 80 ml mixed roasted nuts
- 1 milliliter of kosher salt
- 1.0 ml black pepper

Fish:

- 2 (5-ounce / 142-g) halibut fillets
- 30 mls mayonnaise
- Vegetable oil spray
- Lemon wedges, for serving

Preparation

1. In a small baking pan, mix the coriander, sesame seeds, and cumin to make the dukkah. In the air fryer basket, put the pan. For 5 minutes, preheat the air fryer to 400°F (204°C). You will hear the seeds popping as the cooking process comes to a finish. Put on a plate and allow to cool for five minutes.
2. Add the roasted seeds and mixed nuts to a spice mill or food processor. After cutting coarsely, pulse. Add the salt and pepper, then stir well.
3. Each fish fillet should receive 15ml of mayonnaise. A heaping tablespoon of dukkah should be incorporated into the mayonnaise and lightly pushed into each fillet to ensure adherence.
4. The air fryer basket should be sprayed with vegetable oil. Put the fish in the basket. Set the air fryer to 400°F (204°C) for 12 minutes, or until the salmon flakes easily with a fork.
5. Lemon wedges should be served with fish. Add the roasted seeds and mixed nuts to a spice mill or food processor. After cutting coarsely, pulse. Add the salt and pepper, then stir well.
6. Each fish fillet should receive 15ml of mayonnaise. A heaping tablespoon of dukkah should be incorporated into the mayonnaise and lightly pushed into each fillet to ensure adherence.
7. The air fryer basket should be sprayed with vegetable oil. Put the fish in the basket. Set the air fryer to 400°F (204°C) for 12 minutes, or until the salmon flakes easily with a fork.
8. Lemon wedges should be served with fish.

70. Scallops with Asparagus and Peas

- frying-oil mist
- remove the ends and chop the asparagus into 2-inch pieces, 1 pound (454 g).
- Sugar snap peas, 8 fl. oz.
- 1 pound (454 g) the sea scallop
- Lemon juice, freshly squeezed, 15 ml
- Extra virgin olive oil, 10 ml
- 2.5 mg of dried thyme
- To taste, add salt and freshly ground black pepper.

Preparation

1. Place the crisper plate inside the basket and the basket inside the unit. To preheat the appliance, choose AIR FRY, set the temperature to 400°F (204°C), and set the timer for 3 minutes. Select START/STOP to begin.
2. When the device has warmed up, spray some cooking oil on the crisper plate. Place the asparagus and sugar snap peas in the basket.
3. Set the temperature and timings to 400°F (204°C) after selecting AIR FRY. Select START/STOP to begin.
4. While you wait, look inside the scallops for a little muscle that is attached to the side. Remove it and discard it. In a medium bowl, mix the scallops, lemon juice, olive oil, and thyme. To taste, add salt and pepper.
5. The vegetables should just be beginning to become soft after 3 minutes. Over the vegetables, arrange the scallops. To continue cooking, place the basket back in. Remove the basket and give it a shake after another 3 minutes. Replacing the basket will allow you to continue cooking.
6. The veggies should be soft and the scallops should be firm when tested with a finger and opaque in the center. Serve right away.

Appetizer& Snacks Recipes

71. Roasted Cashews

- Preparation Time: 5 minutes

Ingredients:

- Raw cashew nuts weighing 14 fl. oz.
- Salt and freshly ground black pepper, if needed. 15 ml melted butter

Preparation:

1. Combine all the ingredients in a bowl.
2. Select "Air Fry" mode by turning the dial and pressing the "Power" button on the Digital Air Fry Oven.
3. To adjust the cooking time to 5 minutes, press the TIME/SLICE button and spin the dial once more.
4. Now press the TEMP/DARKNESS button and turn the dial to 355 degrees Fahrenheit.
5. To begin, click the "Start/Pause" button.

6. Open the oven door when the device beeps to indicate that it is preheated.
7. Place the air fry basket with the cashews inside the oven.
8. Midway through, give the cashews a little shake.
9. When the cashews have finished cooking, open the oven door, and place them in a heatproof bowl.
10. Serve hot.

Nutritional Information per Serving:

- Kcal: 202 |Carbs: 11.2g | Fiber: 1g | Sugar: 1.7g | Protein: 5.3g

72. Beef Taquitos

- Preparation Time: 15 minutes

Ingredients:

- 6 tortillas de maiz
- Olive oil cooking spray, 8 fl. oz. of pepper jack cheese, 4 fl. oz. of chopped onion, and 12 fl. oz. of cooked beef.

Preparation:

1. Spread the tortillas out across a flat surface.
2. Each tortilla should have shredded meat in one corner, followed by cheese and onion.
3. To wrap each tortilla and seal the filling, use toothpicks.
4. Evenly coat each taquito with cooking spray.
5. Place the taquitos on the sheet pan that has been oiled.
6. Put the greased sheet pan with the tofu mixture inside.
7. Select "Air Fry" mode by turning the dial and pressing the "Power" button on the Digital Air Fry Oven.
8. To set the cooking time to 8 minutes, press the TIME/SLICE button and spin the dial once more.
9. Now press the TEMP/DARKNESS button and turn the dial to 400 degrees Fahrenheit.
10. To begin, click the "Start/Pause" button.
11. Open the oven door and place the sheet pan inside after the appliance beeps to indicate that it is preheated.
12. Open the oven door after the cooking is finished, then place the taquitos on a dish.

Nutritional Information per Serving:

- Kcal: 228 | Carbs: 12.3g | Fiber: 1.7g | Sugar: 0.6g | Protein: 22.7g

73. Persimmon Chips

- Servings: 2

Ingredients:

- two ripe persimmons, sliced into horizontal slices.
- if needed, salt and freshly ground black pepper

Preparation:

1. Place the persimmon slices on the sheet pan that has been oiled.
2. Select "Air Fry" mode by turning the dial and pressing the "Power" button on the Digital Air Fry Oven.
3. To adjust the cooking time to 10 minutes, press the TIME/SLICE button and spin the dial once more.
4. Now press the TEMP/DARKNESS button and turn the dial to 400 degrees Fahrenheit.
5. To begin, click the "Start/Pause" button.
6. Open the oven door when the device beeps to indicate that it is preheated.
7. Place the baking sheet in the oven.
8. When you're halfway through, turn the chips.
9. Open the oven door after the cooking is finished, then place the chips on a dish.

Nutritional Information per Serving:

- Kcal: 32 | Carbs: 8.4g |

74. Carrot Chips

- Servings: 8

Ingredients:

- 2 pounds of sliced carrots and 59 ml of olive oil
- Sea salt, 15 ml
- 15 milliliters each of ground cinnamon and cumin

Preparation:

1. Sliced carrots should be mixed in a big dish with oil, sea salt, cumin, and cinnamon.
2. Spread the carrot slices in the sheet pan after greasing it.

3. Close the door after transferring the sheet pan to the Digital Air Fry Oven.
4. Rotate the dial to "Bake" mode to select it.
5. Change the setting to 15 minutes by pressing the TIME/SLICE button.
6. Set the temperature to 450 degrees Fahrenheit by pressing the TEMP/DARKNESS button.
7. Press Start/Pause to start the stove.
8. After 7-8 minutes of cooking, turn the chips over and continue baking.

Nutritional Information Per Serving:

- Kcal 182 | Carbs 12.2g | Protein 4.3g

75. Potato Chips

- Servings: 2

Ingredients:

- 15ml of canola oil, 1 medium Russet potato, sliced
- 1.0 ml sea salt
- 1.0 ml black pepper
- 15 ml of freshly chopped rosemary

Preparation:

1. Sliced potatoes should be placed in a nice glass dish filled with cold water.
2. After the potatoes have been left for 20 minutes, drain them. The chips should be dried using a paper towel.
3. Toss the potatoes with oil, salt, and black pepper to evenly coat.
4. In the air fry basket, distribute the potato pieces equally.
5. Close the door after transferring the basket to the Digital Air Fry Oven.
6. Rotate the dial to "Air Fry" to select the mode.
7. Set the value to 25 minutes by pressing the TIME/SLICE button.
8. Set the temperature to 375 degrees Fahrenheit by pressing the TEMP/DARKNESS button.
9. Press Start/Pause to start the stove.
10. rosemary is a nice garnish.

Nutritional Information Per Serving:

- Kcal 134| Carbs 27g | Fiber 3g | Sugar 4g

76. Corn on the Cob

- Servings: 2

Ingredients:

- 2 corn ears
- 30 cc. melted butter
- 2.5 ml of dried parsley
- 1.0 ml sea salt
- Shredded parmesan cheese, 30 ml

Preparation:

1. Both corn ears should be free of silk. Corn can be sliced in half if desired.
2. Melted butter, parsley, and sea salt should all be combined in a mixing bowl. Coat the corn in an equal layer with a pastry brush. Wrap corn with foil if using.
3. Put two rows of corn together inside the sheet pan.
4. It should be put in the oven.
5. Turn on the Digital Air Fry Oven, then select "Air Roast" by rotating the knob.
6. Set the temperature to 350 degrees Fahrenheit and the timer for 12 minutes.
7. To serve hot, remove from the Digital Air Fry Oven.

Nutritional Information per Serving:

- Kcal: 199 |Carbs: 17g | Fiber: 2g | Sugar: 4g |

77. Air Fryer Ravioli

- Servings: 2

Ingredients:

- Frozen ravioli, 12
- Italian breadcrumbs 4 fl oz, 4 fl oz buttermilk
- frying fluid

Preparation:

1. Place two bowls side by side. Put the buttermilk in one and the breadcrumbs in the other.
2. Make sure each ravioli piece is well coated by dipping it in buttermilk, followed by breadcrumbs.
3. Place each breaded ravioli in the air fry basket in a single layer, and spray the tops with oil halfway through.
4. It should be put in the oven.
5. Turn on the digital air fryer and choose "Air Fry" by rotating the knob.
6. Set the temperature to 400 degrees Fahrenheit and the timer for 7 minutes.
7. To serve hot, remove from the digital air fryer.

Nutritional Information per Serving:

- Kcal: 481 | Carbs: 56g | Fiber: 4g

78. Sweet Potato Fries

- Servings: 4

Ingredients:

- 3 fries-sized sweet potatoes
- Olive oil, 30 ml
- 0.5 ml black pepper and 2.5 ml salt
- 2.5 mg of garlic powder

Preparation:

1. French fry-style sweet potato slices should be 1/2 to 1/4 inch thick.
2. The air fry basket should be lightly coated with olive oil cooking spray.
3. In a mixing bowl, add the sweet potatoes and season with the olive oil, salt, pepper, paprika, and garlic powder.
4. Combine them thoroughly to coat them.
5. Each sweet potato fry should be arranged in a single layer in the basket.
6. Put there in the oven.
7. Turn on the digital air fryer and choose "Air Broil" by rotating the knob.
8. Choose the 12-minute unit at LO.

Nutritional Information per Serving:

- Kcal: 230 Carbs: 30g | Fiber: 4g

79. Pasta Chips

- Servings: 4

Ingredients:

- Olive oil, 7.50 ml
- 7.5 ml nutrition yeast
- 8 ounces of bow-tie pasta
- Italian seasoning, 2/3 teaspoon Blend
- A milliliter of salt

Preparation:

1. In half the time specified on the package, cook and boil the pasta in salted water, then drain it.
2. In a bowl, combine the cooked pasta with the nutritional yeast, olive oil, salt, and Italian seasoning.
3. In the air fry basket, spread out this spaghetti.
4. Close the door after moving the basket to the digital air fryer.
5. Rotate the dial to "Air Fry" to select the mode.
6. Set the value to 5 minutes by pressing the TIME/SLICE button.
7. Set the temperature to 390 degrees Fahrenheit by pressing the TEMP/DARKNESS button.
8. Press Start/Pause to start the stove.
9. Toss the pasta, then cook it in the air for a further five minutes.

Nutritional Information Per Serving:

- Kcal 167 | Carbs 26g | Fiber 2g

80. Avocado Fries

- Servings: 4

Ingredients:

- Panko breadcrumbs, 4 fl. oz.
- Salt, 2.5 ml
- Sliced, pitted, and peeled avocado, one
- 8 fl. oz. of whisked egg

Preparation:

1. Salt and breadcrumbs should be combined in a small basin.
2. The avocado strips should first be covered in panko before being dipped in the egg.
3. In the air fryer basket, spread out these slices.
4. Close the door after placing the sandwich inside the digital air fryer.
5. Rotate the dial to "Bake" mode to select it.
6. Change the setting to 20 minutes by pressing the TIME/SLICE button.
7. Set the temperature to 400 degrees Fahrenheit by pressing the TEMP/DARKNESS button.
8. Press Start/Pause to start the stove.

Nutritional Information Per Serving:

- Kcal 110 | Carbs 19g | Fiber 5g

81. Fiesta Chicken Fingers

- Servings: 4

Ingredients:

- 3/4 pound of cut-up, boneless chicken breasts
- 4 fluid ounces buttermilk
- 8 fl. oz. all-purpose flour, 1 ml. pepper
- 3 cups of crumbled corn chips.
- one packet of taco seasoning

Preparation:

1. Sprinkle flour and pepper on the chicken.
2. Combine taco spice with corn chips.
3. Buttermilk is used to coat the chicken fingers before being covered in corn chips.
4. Spray cooking oil on the air fryer basket before adding the chicken fingers.
5. Close the door after moving the basket to the digital air fryer.
6. Rotate the dial to "Air Fry" to select the mode.
7. Change the setting to 12 minutes by pressing the TIME/SLICE button.
8. Set the temperature to 325 degrees Fahrenheit by pressing the TEMP/DARKNESS button.
9. Press Start/Pause to start the stove.
10. Halfway through cooking, flip the chicken fingers, and then continue to cook.
11. Serve warm with fresh salsa or sour cream ranch dip.

Nutritional Information Per Serving:

- Kcal 218 | Carbs 44g | Fiber 5g

Vegetarian & Vegan Recipes

82. Broccoli Stuffed With Cheese And Pepper

- Servings: 4

Ingredients:

- 4 eggs
- 2 medium bell peppers, cut in half, and seeded
- dried sage in 5 ml
- Shredded cheddar cheese, 2.5 ounces
- Almond milk, 7 ounces
- Baby broccoli florets, 2 oz.
- Two-fluid-ounce cherry tomatoes
- spices, salt

Directions:

1. Set the air fryer's temperature to 370°F.
2. Eggs, milk, broccoli, cherry tomatoes, sage, pepper, and salt should all be combined in a mixing dish.
3. Apply frying oil to the air fryer basket using a cooking spray.
4. Fill the air fryer basket with the bell pepper halves.

5. Put the bell pepper halves with the egg mixture inside.
6. After adding cheese, roast the bell pepper for 20 minutes..

83. Healthy Veggie Rice

- Servings: 2

Ingredients:

- cooked white rice weighing 12 ounces
- Lightly beaten, one large egg
- 4 fl. oz. of frozen peas, 4 fl. oz. of frozen carrots, 2.5 ml. of thawed sesame seeds, and 15 ml. of vegetable oil
- 15 ml of water, 30 ml of toasted sesame oil, and
- as needed, salt and freshly ground white pepper
- Soy sauce, 5 ml.
- Sriracha sauce, 5 ml.

Directions:

1. Set the air fryer to 380 degrees Fahrenheit to get it ready. Use cooking oil to grease the pan.
2. In a bowl, combine the rice with the vegetable oil, salt, white pepper, 5 ml of sesame oil, and water.
3. Cook the rice mixture for 12 minutes after transferring it to the air fryer basket.
4. Cook the rice for a few minutes after adding the beaten egg.
5. Add the carrots and peas. Cook for a further two minutes.
6. In the meantime, combine the remaining sesame oil, soy sauce, Sriracha sauce, sesame seeds, and a bowl.
7. Potato cubes should be placed on serving platters with sauce drizzled over them.

84. Sweet And Spicy Tofu

- Servings: 3

Ingredients:

- For Tofu:
- 1 (14-ounces) block firm tofu, pressed and cubed
- 4 fl. oz arrowroot flour
- 2.5 ml. sesame oil

For Sauce:

- Low-sodium soy sauce in 60 ml
- Rice vinegar, 1 1/30 milliliter
- Chile sauce, 1 1/30 ml.
- Agave nectar in 15 ml
- 5 ml of minced garlic from 2 large cloves. freshly cut, peeled, and shredded ginger
- 2 minced chives (green portion).

Directions:

1. The arrowroot flour, tofu, and sesame oil should all be combined in a dish.
2. Set the air fryer's temperature to 360°F. Grease an air fryer basket liberally.
3. Put the tofu pieces in a single layer in the air fryer basket that has been prepared.
4. Cook in the air for about 20 minutes, shaking once.
5. Regarding the sauce, put all the ingredients in a plate. Do not use the chives. When well blended, beat it.
6. Take the tofu out of the air fryer and place it in a skillet with the sauce. Cook over medium heat for about 3 minutes, stirring occasionally.
7. Serve heated with chives as a garnish.

85. Delicious Vegan Calzone

- Servings: 1

Ingredients:

- Olive oil, 5 ml
- minced 1/2 a little onion
- 2 sliced and seeded sweet peppers
- Sea salt for improved flavor
- peppercorns, ground, 1 milliliter
- Dry oregano, 1 milliliter
- Prepared Italian pizza dough weighing 4 ounces
- 2.2 ounces of marinara sauce
- 2 ounces of vegan cheese shreds of mozzarella

Directions:

1. Use a heated, nonstick pan and add oil. Once hot, sauté the onion and peppers for about 5 minutes, or until they are fragrant and soft. Include oregano, black pepper, and salt.
2. Pizza dough should be rolled out on a kitchen counter after being dusted with flour.
3. Add the sautéed mixture, vegan cheese, and marinara sauce to the top half of the dough. Create a pocket by folding the dough over gently and sealing the edges.
4. To make a few holes in the dough, use a fork. Place in the frying basket that has been lightly greased after adding a few drizzles of olive oil.
5. The calzones should be baked in the preheated air fryer at 330°F for 12 minutes, turning them over halfway through. Good appetite!

86. Tofu Ala Italian

- Servings: 2
- Prep & Cooking Time: 30 Minutes

Ingredients:

- Black pepper for better taste
- 15 ml. vegetable broth
- 15 ml. soy sauce
- 1.5 ml. dried oregano
- 1.5 ml. garlic powder
- 1.5 ml. dried basil
- 1.5 ml. onion powder

Directions:

1. Cut the tofu into three even squares along the length. Tofu should be placed on one side of the cutting board that has been lined with paper towels before being covered. Gently press the tofu with your hands to release as much liquid as you can.
2. Take off the paper towels and cut the tofu into 8 cubes using a knife. Set aside. Combine the soy sauce, vegetable broth, oregano, basil, garlic powder, onion powder, and black pepper in a separate bowl by stirring everything together with a spoon.
3. The tofu should be thoroughly coated with the spice mixture before being let 10 minutes to marinate. Set the tofu in the air fryer's basket in a single layer, preheat to 380°F, and cook for 10 minutes, turning it over after six minutes.
4. Place on a dish and accompany with a green salad.

87. Stuffed Eggplant With A Twist

- Servings: 4

Ingredients:

- 8 baby eggplants
- 60 ml. olive oil, divided
- 3/4 tbsp. dry mango powder
- 3/4 tbsp. ground coriander
- 2.5 ml. ground cumin
- 2.5 ml. ground turmeric
- 2.5 ml. garlic powder
- Salt for better taste

Directions:

1. Before putting oil in the fryer basket, preheat the air fryer to 370°F.
2. Each eggplant's stem should remain intact as you cut incisions from the bottom.
3. Fill each eggplant slit with the mixture made by combining one teaspoon of oil with the spices in a basin.
4. Place the eggplants in the air fryer basket after brushing the outside of each one with the leftover oil.
5. Cook for approximately 12 minutes, then transfer to a serving plate to keep warm.

88. Glazed Carrots

- Servings: 4

Ingredients:

- 3 cups carrots, peeled and divided into large chunks
- 15 ml. olive oil
- 15 ml. honey
- Salt & black pepper for better taste

Directions:

1. Before putting oil in the fryer basket, preheat the air fryer to 390°F.
2. In a bowl, combine all the ingredients and toss to thoroughly coat.
3. Cook for 12 minutes after transferring to the air fryer basket.
4. Serve while still heated.

89. Veggies Air-Fried Sushi

- Servings: 4
- Prep & Cooking Time: 60 Minutes

Ingredients:

- 4 nori sheets
- 1 carrot, sliced lengthways
- 1 red bell pepper, seeds removed, sliced
- 1 avocado, sliced
- 15 ml. olive oil mixed with
- 15 ml. rice wine vinegar
- 8 fl.oz panko crumbs
- 30 mls. sesame seeds
- Serve it with soy sauce or wasabi. Add picked ginger as desired.

Directions:

1. Prepare a sushi mat, a small dish of lukewarm water, and a clean work surface. Wet your hands, place a nori sheet on a sushi mat, top with half a cup of sushi rice, and leave a half-inch border around the nori so you can roll it up.

2. Aside from the rice, arrange the avocado, pepper, and carrot. To seal the sushi, roll it tightly and run a warm water rag along the nori strip.
3. Combine oil and rice vinegar in a bowl. Mix the crumbs and sesame seeds in a separate bowl. Each sushi log should be rolled in the vinegar mixture before going directly to the sesame bowl to be coated.
4. Sushi should be placed in the air fryer and cooked for 14 minutes at 360°F while being turned once.
5. Slice and serve with wasabi, ginger pickles, and soy sauce.

90. Drizzling Onion

- Servings: 4
- Prep & Cooking Time: 20 Minutes

Ingredients:

- Olive oil as needed
- 5 ml. cayenne pepper
- 5 ml. garlic powder
- 12 fl .oz flour
- 15 ml. pepper
- 15 ml. paprika
- 15 ml. salt
- 2 fl .oz mayonnaise
- 15 ml. ketchup
- 2 fl .oz mayonnaise
- 2 fl .oz kefir

Directions:

1. Combine salt, pepper, paprika, flour, garlic powder, and cayenne pepper in a mixing bowl. Stir in the kefir, mayonnaise, and ketchup to the mixture.
2. Apply the prepared mixture on the onions and then mist with oil.
3. Your air fryer should first be heated to 360°F. 15 minutes should be spent cooking the coated onions in the basket.

91. Eggplant Potato And Zucchini Chips

- Servings: 4
- Prep & Cooking Time: 10 Minutes

Ingredients:

- 5 potatoes, divided strips
- 3 zucchinis, divided into strips
- 4 fl. oz cornstarch
- 4 fl. oz water
- 4 fl. oz olive oil
- Salt to season

Directions:

1. Turn on air fryer and heat to 390°F. Combine cornstarch, water, salt, pepper, oil, potatoes, eggplants, and zucchini in a mixing bowl.
2. In the basket of the fryer, put one-third of the vegetable strips, and cook them for five minutes while shaking the pan once.
3. Transfer them to a platter once they are ready. Serve hot.

92. Baked Potato And Parsnip

- Servings: 8
- Prep & Cooking Time: 30 Minutes

Ingredients:

- 3 tbsps. pine nuts
- 28 ounces parsnips, minced
- 1 3/4 ounces coarsely minced Parmesan cheese
- 6 3/4 ouncse crème fraiche
- 1 slice bread
- 30 mls. sage
- 60 ml. butter
- 60 ml. mustard

Directions:

1. Preheat Air Fryer To 360°F. Put Salted Water In A Pot Over Medium Heat. Add Potatoes And Parsnips. Bring To A Boil For 10 Minutes.
2. In A Bowl, Mix Mustard, Crème Fraiche, Sage, Salt And Pepper. Leave The Potatoes And Parsnips To Dry And Mash With The Milk, Salt, Butter, Black Pepper, And Cayenne Pepper.
3. Add Mustard Mixture, Bread, Cheese, And Nuts To The Mash And Mix. Add The Batter To Your Air Fryer's Basket And Cook For 15 Minutes, Shaking Once. Serve.

93. Cheesy Pizza With A Crust Made Of Broccoli

- Servings: 1

Ingredients:

- 3 cups of steaming broccoli rice
- 4 fl. oz. of grated parmesan cheese
- 1 egg
- Low-carb Alfredo sauce, 3 tablespoons
- 4 fl. oz. of grated parmesan cheese

Directions:

1. In a bowl, thoroughly mix the drained broccoli rice with the Parmesan cheese and egg.
2. Cut a piece of parchment paper that is about the same size as the basket base of the deep-fat fryer. Four evenly sized spoonfuls of the broccoli mixture should be placed on the paper. Each spoonful should be pressed into the shape of a pizza crust. This section might need to be finished in two groups. the fryer after moving the parchment there.
3. Cook for five minutes at 280 °F. Turn it over when the crust has firmed up and cook for an additional two minutes.
4. On top of the crusts, add the Alfredo sauce and mozzarella cheese, and simmer for an additional seven minutes. When the cheese and sauce have melted, the crusts are prepared. Serve warm.

Dessert Recipes

94. Apple Pastries

Ingredients:

- Peeled, cored, and cut one-half of a large apple.
- 15 milliliters of freshly grated orange zest
- White sugar, 7.50 ml
- 2.5 ml of cinnamon, ground
- Prepared frozen puff pastry weighing 7.05 ounces.

Preparation:

1. Combine all ingredients—except puff pastry—in a bowl.
2. 16 squares of pastry should be cut.
3. A spoonful or so of the apple mixture should go in the middle of each square.
4. With damp fingers, gently press the edges of each square as it is folded into a triangle.
5. After that, firmly push the edges with a fork.
6. Turn the dial to "Air Fry" mode on the Digital Air Fry Oven and press the "Power" button.
7. To adjust the cooking time to 10 minutes, press the TIME/SLICE button and spin the dial once more.
8. Now press the TEMP/DARKNESS button and turn the dial to 390 degrees Fahrenheit.

9. To begin, click the "Start/Pause" button.
10. Open the oven door when the device beeps to indicate that it is preheated.
11. Placing the pastries in the oven after greasing the air fryer basket.
12. Open the oven door after the baking period is through, then remove the pastries and place them on a dish.

Nutritional Information per Serving:

- Kcal: 198 | Carbs: 18.8g | Protein: 2.5g

95. Blueberry Hand Pies

Ingredients:

- 8 fl.oz blueberries
- 27.5 mls caster sugar
- 15 ml lemon juice
- 1 pinch salt
- 320g refrigerated pie crust
- Water

Preparation:

1. In a medium mixing dish, combine the blueberries, sugar, lemon juice, and salt.
2. Cut out six to eight distinct rounds from the rolled pie crusts (4 inches).
3. Place around 1 spoonful of the blueberry filling in the middle of each circle.
4. To form a half-moon, wet the dough's edges and fold them over the filling.
5. Use a fork to gently crimp the piecrust's edges together. Next, make three slits in the hand pies' tops.
6. The hand pies should be covered in cooking oil.
7. Put them on the baking sheet.
8. Turn on the Digital Air Fry Oven, then select "Bake" by rotating the knob.
9. Set the temperature to 350 degrees Fahrenheit and the timer for 20 minutes.
10. Before serving, let the food cool for two minutes.

Nutritional Information per Serving:

- Kcal: 251 | Carbs: 30g | Fiber: 1g |

96. Brownie Bars

Ingredients:

Brownie:

- 4 fl oz of diced butter.
- Two large, beaten eggs and one ounce of unsweetened chocolate.
- 20 ml of vanilla extract
- 8 ounces of sugar
- All-purpose flour, 8 fl. oz.
- 30 grams of baking powder
- 8 fl. oz. chopped walnuts

Filling

- 6 ounces of softened cream cheese and 4 fl. oz. of sugar
- 30 mls of all-purpose flour and 59 mls of softened butter
- 2.5 cc of vanilla extract and 1 big beaten egg

Topping

- 6 ounces of chocolate chips in 8 fl. oz.
- 12 fl oz of small marshmallows and 8 fl oz of chopped walnuts

Frosting

- 60 ml of butter
- 60 ml of milk
- Cream cheese, 2 ounces
- Unsweetened chocolate, 1 ounce
- 3 cups of sugar for sweets
- 20 ml of vanilla extract

Preparation:

1. Add all the filling ingredients to a small bowl and stir until combined.
2. Melt the butter and chocolate together in a big pot over medium heat.
3. Mix thoroughly, then turn off the heat source for the melted chocolate.
4. Then mix thoroughly while adding the vanilla, eggs, baking powder, flour, sugar, and nuts.

5. In the sheet pan, spread this chocolate batter.
6. Sprinkle the batter with nuts, marshmallows, and chocolate chips.
7. Close the door after placing the pan inside the Digital Air Fry Oven.
8. Rotate the dial to "Air Fry" to select the mode.
9. Change the setting to 28 minutes by pressing the TIME/SLICE button.
10. Set the temperature to 350 degrees Fahrenheit by pressing the TEMP/DARKNESS button.
11. Press Start/Pause to start the stove.
12. Butter, cream cheese, chocolate, and milk are heated in a good saucepan over medium heat to make the frosting.
13. After thoroughly combining, turn off the heat.
14. Add sugar and vanilla after thoroughly mixing.
15. Over the brownie, spread this icing.
16. Slice the brownie into bars after it has cooled.

Nutritional Information Per Serving:

- Kcal 298 | Carbs 34g | Fiber 1g

97. Vanilla Soufflé

Ingredients:

- 59 ml softened butter
- 59 ml all-purpose flour, 4 fl oz of sugar, and 8 fl oz of milk, divided.
- 15 ml split vanilla extract
- four egg yolks
- five egg whites
- Cream of tartar, 15 ml
- Extra powdered sugar for dusting is added to the 30 cc.

Preparation:

1. Butter and flour should be combined in a bowl until a homogeneous paste formed.
2. 4 fl. oz. of sugar and milk should be combined in a medium pan and heated over low heat while being continually stirred for about 3 minutes, or until the sugar is dissolved.
3. Stirring continually, add the flour mixture and simmer for 3–4 minutes, or until the sauce thickens.
4. Add 15 cc of vanilla essence after taking the pan off the heat.
5. Allow to cool for about 10 minutes.
6. The egg yolks and 15 ml of vanilla essence should be combined well in a bowl.
7. Once blended, add the egg yolk mixture to the milk mixture.
8. The egg whites, cream of tartar, remaining sugar, and vanilla essence should all be combined in a separate basin and whisked together until stiff peaks form.
9. Mixture of milk and egg whites should be incorporated.
10. Six ramekins should be greased and dusted with a little sugar.
11. Place the mixture into the prepared ramekins, and level the top with the back of a spoon.
12. Turn the dial to "Air Fry" mode on the Digital Air Fry Oven and press the "Power" button.
13. To set the cooking time to 16 minutes, press the TIME/SLICE button and spin the dial once more.
14. Now press the TEMP/DARKNESS button and turn the dial to 330 degrees Fahrenheit.
15. To begin, click the "Start/Pause" button.
16. Open the oven door when the device beeps to indicate that it is preheated.
17. Insert the air fry basket with the ramekins into the oven.
18. Open the oven door after the cooking process is finished, then set the ramekins onto a wire rack to cool somewhat.
19. Serve warm and top with powdered sugar.

Nutritional Information per Serving:

- Kcal: 250 | Carbs: 29.8g | Protein: 6.8g

98. Chocolate Chip Cookie

Ingredients:

- 4 fl. oz butter, softened
- 4 fl. oz sugar
- 4 fl. oz brown sugar
- 1 egg
- 15 ml vanilla
- 2.5 mls baking soda
- 1 mls salt
- 12 fl. ozs all-purpose flour
- 8 fl.oz chocolate chips

Preparation:

1. Spray cooking oil on the sheet pan to grease it.
2. In a mixing dish, combine butter, white sugar, and brown sugar.
3. Mix thoroughly after adding the vanilla, egg, salt, flour, and baking soda.
4. After adding the chocolate chips, gently knead the dough.
5. In the sheet pan, evenly distribute the prepared dough.
6. Close the door after placing the pan inside the Digital Air Fry Oven.
7. Rotate the dial to "Bake" mode to select it.
8. Change the setting to 12 minutes by pressing the TIME/SLICE button.
9. Set the temperature to 400 degrees Fahrenheit by pressing the TEMP/DARKNESS button.
10. Press Start/Pause to start the stove.

Nutritional Information Per Serving:

- Kcal 173 | Carbs 24.8g | Fiber 1.1g | Sugar 18g | Protein 15g

99. Air Fried Butter Cake

Ingredients:

- frying oil
- Butter in 75 g
- White sugar in 59 ml plus 30 ml
- 18 fluid ounces all-purpose flour, 1 egg
- 1 dash of salt
- Milk, 90 ml

Preparation:

1. Choose the AIR FRY setting for 15 minutes at 350°F. Spray cooking oil in a small fluted tube pan that can be used in an air fryer.
2. Using an electric mixer, first combine the sugar and the butter. Add the egg after it's light and creamy, then continue mixing until the batter is smooth and fluffy.
3. Add the milk and thoroughly combine the batter after adding the flour and salt. With the back of a spoon, spread the batter evenly in the preheated pan.
4. The air fryer should have a pan in it. For roughly 15 minutes, bake it. Before removing the cake from the pan, let it cool for about five minutes.

Nutritional Information Per Serving:

- Kcal: 470 | Carbs: 59.7g | Protein: 7.7g

100. Shortbread Fingers

Ingredients:

- 4 fl.oz caster sugar
- 18 fl .Oz's plain flour
- 177 ml butter

Preparation:

1. Mix the flour and sugar in a large bowl.
2. When a smooth dough forms, add the butter and continue mixing.
3. Cut the dough into 10 fingers of the same size.
4. Lightly puncture the fingertips with a fork.
5. Put the fingers in the sheet pan that has been lightly greased.
6. Select "Air Fry" mode by turning the dial and pressing the "Power" button on the Digital Air Fry Oven.
7. To set the cooking time to 12 minutes, press the TIME/SLICE button and spin the dial once more.
8. Now press the TEMP/DARKNESS button and turn the dial to 355 degrees Fahrenheit.
9. To begin, click the "Start/Pause" button.
10. Open the oven door when the device beeps to indicate that it is preheated.
11. Insert the pan in the oven with the air fryer basket in place.
12. Open the oven door after the cooking is finished, then set the baking pan onto a wire rack to cool for about 5 to 10 minutes.
13. The shortbread fingers should now be turned over onto the wire rack to finish cooling before serving.

Nutritional Information per Serving:

- Kcal: 223 | Carbs: 22.6g |Protein: 2.3g

Conclusion

The greatest method for cooking without covering your kitchen top with oil is the air fryer. Everyone wants to lead a healthy lifestyle, but eating bland food will make you sick and won't be able to quell your appetite. Therefore, eating pleasant food is essential. The topic of where to find delicious cuisine without sacrificing health emerges. The Air Fryer is the remedy for the modern day. Because there is little to no oil used during the cooking process, air-fried food is excellent, flavorful, and low in calories. The texture of air-fried food is identical to that of roasted or baked food.

This fantastic cookbook will provide you with comprehensive advice on air frying and healthy living. You may spend less time in the kitchen and always have delicious cuisine without sacrificing flavor. With the aid of this wonderful book and the Air Fryer, you may indulge in all your food addictions without feeling guilty about being overweight.

You will plan healthy parties and wow your family and friends with your food with the help of this book. If you're trying to lose weight, now is the time to pick up this cookbook and your preferred Air Fryer and start enjoying your diet.

Appendix 1
Measurement Conversion Chart

- **WEIGHT EQUIVALENTS**

US STANDARD	METRIC (APPROXIMATE)
1 ounce	28 g
2 ounces	57 g
5 ounces	142 g
10 ounces	284 g
15 ounces	425 g
16 ounces (1 pound)	455 g
1.5 pounds	680 g
2 pounds	907 g

- **VOLUME EQUIVALENTS (LIQUID)**

US STANDARD	US STANDARD (OUNCES)	METRIC (APPROXIMATE)
30 mls	1 fl.oz	30 mL
59 ml	2 fl.oz	60 mL
4 fl. oz	4 fl.oz	120 mL
8 fl.oz	8 fl.oz	240 mL
14 fl. oz	12 fl.oz	355 mL
12 fl.oz or 1 pint	16 fl.oz	475 mL
4 cups or 1 quart	32 fl.oz	1 L
1 gallon	128 fl.oz	4 L

- **VOLUME EQUIVALENTS (DRY)**

US STANDARD	METRIC (APPROXIMATE)
⅛ teaspoon	0.5 mL
1 ml	1 mL
2.5 ml	2 mL
7.5 ml	4 mL
15 ml	5 mL
15 ml	15 mL
59 ml	59 mL
4 fl. oz	118 mL
177 ml	177 mL
8 fl.oz	235 mL
12 fl.oz	475 mL
3 cups	700 mL
4 cups	1 L

- **TEMPERATURES EQUIVALENTS**

FAHRENHEIT(F)	CELSIUS(C) (APPROXIMATE)
225	107
250	120
275	135
300	150
325	160
350	180
375	190
400	205
425	220
450	235
475	245
500	260

Printed in Great Britain
by Amazon

29222112R00057